POWER
FAITH

JACK W. HAYFORD
Executive Editor

THOMAS NELSON
Since 1798

NASHVILLE   DALLAS   MEXICO CITY   RIO DE JANEIRO

D0112047

Published in Nashville, Tennessee, by Thomas Nelson. Thomas Nelson is a registered trademark of Thomas Nelson, Inc.

Thomas Nelson, Inc., titles may be purchased in bulk for educational, business, fund-raising, or sales promotional use. For information, please e-mail SpecialMarkets@ThomasNelson.com.

Hayford, Jack W.

Power Faith

ISBN-13: 978-1-4185-4858-2

Printed in the United States of America

11 12 13 14 15 [QG] 6 5 4 3 2 1

TABLE OF CONTENTS

A Balanced View

Every believer knows what it means to struggle with faith—wondering if greater trust in God would result in greater effectiveness in the kingdom. Perhaps the Apostle Paul was referring to this struggle *p. 1055* when he used the phrase, "the good fight of faith" (1 Timothy 6:12). For *is → Progress* him, faith's struggle was not merely in matters of ministry but referred *Faith is the gift of God Eph. 2:8* more to the whole of his relationship with the Lord Jesus. Writing from a jail cell at the end of his life, aware that he could be summoned at any moment to his execution, Paul admits that faith has been a fight, albeit a *good* one.

In order to effectively engage in this battle and prevail in this ongoing struggle to walk by faith it is important to recognize these facts regarding "the good fight of faith":

- *Anything done without faith cannot please God (Hebrews 11:6).* *P. 1065*
- *Grace can be accessed only by faith (Ephesians 2:8).* *1838*
- *Every person has the capacity for faith (Romans 12:3).* *1008 "a measure of faith"*
- *Faith is one of the gifts of the Holy Spirit (1 Corinthians 12:7–11).* *1020*
- *Nothing is impossible when you have even the smallest faith (Matthew 17:14–21).* *P 866 - 7*

During this study in God's Word, you will consider many important faith questions:

- Can I ask God for anything, and as long as I have the right faith, get what I ask for?
- If I believe, can I have assurance that my children will be saved?
- Does faith guarantee that I will never have to deal with sickness or pain?
- Is there ever a time when my lack of faith might make God angry? If I make Him mad, am I still saved?

Together, "let us draw near with a true heart in full assurance of faith" (Hebrews 10:22) and find faith's *way* according to God's *Word*!

Keys of the Kingdom

KEYS CAN BE SYMBOLS of possession, of the right and ability to acquire, clarify, open or ignite. Keys can be concepts that unleash mind-boggling possibilities. Keys clear the way to a possibility otherwise obstructed!

Jesus spoke of keys: "And I will give you the keys of the kingdom of heaven, and whatever you bind on earth will be bound in heaven, and whatever you loose on earth will be loosed in heaven" (Matthew. 16:19).

While Jesus did not define the "keys" He has given, it is clear that He did confer specific tools upon His church which grant us access to a realm of spiritual "partnership" with Him. The "keys" are concepts or biblical themes, traceable throughout Scripture, which are verifiably dynamic when applied with solid faith under the lordship of Jesus Christ. The "partnership" is the essential feature of this enabling grace; allowing believers to receive Christ's promise of "kingdom keys," and to be assured of the Holy Spirit's readiness to actuate their power in the life of the believer.

Faithful students of the Word of God, and some of today's most respected Christian leaders, have noted some of the primary themes which undergird this spiritual partnership. A concise presentation of many of these primary themes can be found in the Kingdom Dynamics feature of *The New Spirit-Filled Life Bible*. The *New Spirit-Filled Life Study Guide Series*, an outgrowth of this Kingdom Dynamics feature, provides a treasury of more in-depth insights on these central truths. This study series offers challenges and insights designed to enable you to more readily understand and appropriate certain dynamic "Kingdom Keys."

Each study guide has twelve to fourteen lessons, and a number of helpful features have been developed to assist you in your study, each marked by a symbol and heading for easy identification.

Kingdom Key

KINGDOM KEY identifies the foundational Scripture passage for each study session and highlights a basic concept or principle presented in the text along with cross-referenced passages.

Kingdom Life

The KINGDOM LIFE feature is designed to give practical understanding and insight. This feature will assist you in comprehending the truths contained in Scripture and applying them to your day-to-day needs, hurts, relationships, concerns, or circumstances.

Word Wealth

The WORD WEALTH feature provides important definitions of key terms.

Behind the Scenes

BEHIND THE SCENES supplies information about cultural beliefs and practices, doctrinal disputes, and various types of background information that will illuminate Bible passages and teachings.

Kingdom Extra

The optional KINGDOM EXTRA feature will guide you to Bible dictionaries, Bible encyclopedias, and other resources that will enable you to gain further insight into a given topic.

Probing the Depths

Finally, PROBING THE DEPTHS will present any controversial issues raised by particular lessons and may cite Bible passages or other sources to assist you in arriving at your own conclusions.

This Spirit-Filled Life Study Guide is a comprehensive resource presenting study and life-application questions and exercises with spaces provided to record your answers. These study guides are designed to provide all you need to gain a good, basic understanding of the covered theme and apply biblical counsel to your life. You will need only a heart and mind open to the Holy Spirit, a prayerful attitude, a pencil and a Bible to complete the studies and apply the truths they contain. However, you may want to have a notebook handy if you plan to expand your study to include the optional Kingdom Extra feature.

The Bible study method used in this series employs four basic steps:

1. *Observation:* What does the text say?
2. *Interpretation:* What is the original meaning of the text?
3. *Correlation:* What light can be shed on this text by other Scripture passages?
4. *Application:* How should my life change in response to the Holy Spirit's teaching of this text?

The New King James Version is the translation used wherever Scripture portions are cited in the *New Spirit-Filled Life Study Guide* series. Using this translation with this series will make your study easier, but it is certainly not imperative, and you will profit through use of any translation you choose.

Through Bible study, you will grow in your essential understanding of the Lord, His kingdom and your place in it; but you need more. Jesus was sent to teach us "all things" (John 14:26; 1 Corinthians 2:13). Rely on the Holy Spirit to guide your study and your application of the Bible's truths. Bathe your study time in prayer as you use this series to learn of Him and His plan for your life. Ask the Spirit of God to illuminate the text, enlighten your mind, humble your will, and comfort your heart. And as you explore the Word of God and find the keys to unlock its riches, may the Holy Spirit fill every fiber of your being with the joy and power God longs to give all His children. Read diligently on. Stay open and submissive to Him. Learn to live your life as the Creator intended. You will not be disappointed. He promises you!

SESSION ONE

Examples of Faith

Philippians 3:17 Brethren, join in following my example, and note those who so walk, as you have us for a pattern.

The Greek word *summimetes* (Strong's #4831) is translated in this passage as "join in following my example." It can be understood to mean "become imitators of me." Throughout Scripture, we are given examples of strong, sure faith. These examples provide us with a pattern to follow, a model to which we are to aspire. Our biblical predecessors in the walk of faith can act as our guides as we learn to live the life of faith.

Another word in this short passage that is pivotal to our understanding is "pattern"; it is derived from the Greek word *tupos* (with the root word *tupto*) meaning to strike an exact pattern as with a metal die. So we're not left with only a shadow or a hint of a path to follow—we have a solid pattern we can strive to match. One that is clear and intentional.

The sense of this passage is one of replication and continuity—not in an effort to destroy diversity in the kingdom, but to continually recreate within God's people the strong, sure walk of faith modeled by the faithful who have gone before—the same walk to which we all are called. The walk of power faith!

Read Hebrews 11.

Questions:

This chapter is often called "the faith chapter" of the Bible. How does reading this account of the faithful impact your faith?

_____

_____

_____

The people mentioned in this passage are often referred to as "heroes of faith." What about their lives made them "heroic"?

_____

_____

What are the characteristics that are common to each of the people mentioned in these examples of faith-filled lives?

_____

_____

What steps can you take to incorporate these characteristics into your own life?

_____

_____

 Word Wealth—*Overcome*

Overcome, *nike* (neeh´-kay); Strong's #3528, 3529: This Greek word is also the name of the goddess of victory in Greek mythology. But military or athletic victory that focuses only on human goals is as insubstantial as the myth from which the word is derived. What is real and what has substance is this: When you put your faith in the Son of God—when you become one born of God—your faith then makes you an overcomer and gives you a victory that can never be taken away from you!

Probing the Depths

1 John 5:4 says, ". . . and this is the victory that has overcome the world—our faith." But at what point is the victory yours? When do you become an "overcomer"?

Our society suggests that the experience of victory can only be real when you have *what* you want *when* you want it. But the Bible teaches that you win, not when you get what you want, but *the moment you believe!* If you are surrounded by problems, victory doesn't wait until they're solved, but arrives the moment you believe that God will sustain you through or beyond them. If you are sick, you win over sickness the moment you believe in God's promise that Jesus Christ is your Healer—when this promise becomes alive and real to you. If you find yourself in poverty, you win the moment you believe what God has said about your financial circumstances. You become an overcomer the moment you place your faith in the Son of God, and what His Word is speaking into your life.

Read Romans 8:31–39; Revelation 3:10–12; Hebrews 11:1.

Questions:

In your opinion, in what ways are the terms "more than conquerors" and "overcomers" related?

✎ _____

_____

_____

What is your understanding of Jesus' promises to the faithful in Revelation 3? In what way should these promises affect your life today?

✎ _____

_____

_____

Considering the definition of faith in Hebrews 11, in what ways do you think this understanding can lead you to victorious life as an overcomer?

✎ _____

_____

_____

 Kingdom Life—*Faith That Pleases God*

In Hebrews 11:6, we read: "But without faith it is impossible to please Him, for he who comes to God must believe that He is, and that He is a rewarder of those who diligently seek Him." According to this verse, faith that pleases God does three things:

- *Pleasing faith comes actively before God*—"those who diligently seek Him." To be diligent, as it is used here, means to investigate, crave, or demand. It is an insistent coming. Nothing in this graphic, word picture is intended to portray someone nagging God! However, Jesus Himself taught about the importance of this diligent, aggressive, seeking attitude in prayer.

Read Luke 11:5–10.

Questions:

What insight do you gain from this parable?

✎ _____

_____

_____

What understanding can be gleaned from the meaning of the word "diligent"? How can you incorporate this attitude into your prayer life?

✎ _____

_____

This passage conveys a desired boldness in our approach to God. How is this different from mere tenacity?

✎ _____

_____

- *Pleasing faith believes God exists*—"believe[s] that He is." Some people's prayers sound as though they are talking to themselves! Have you ever prayed without even thinking of standing in His presence? God wants your faith to focus on the reality of His being. Contrary to modern world views, God *is* there!—and He insists that you think so in order to please Him.

  For most of us, this is theoretically not an issue. As Christians, we have already professed faith in God through Christ. In that sense, we believe He exists. The problem comes when we're under pressure. Do we believe He exists in these troubling circumstances? That's when your faith pleases God—when by faith you can see Him *in* your situation.

Read James 2:19.

Questions:

What is the difference between simple belief and true faith?

✎ _____

_____

- *Pleasing faith believes God is a rewarder*—"and that He is a rewarder." In some cultures, this word might simply mean a good employer. It has the sense of wages or money given for hire. If it were only to mean that, then God is pleased when you believe. He's a good boss! But it's much more than believing God gives good wages. "Rewarder" has the meaning of beyond recompense, of reimbursing beyond the value of what was received. Pleasing faith believes God rewards beyond normal recompense when He is diligently sought.

Read Ephesians 3:20–21.

Questions:

In what way do your expectations of God reveal your perception of Him?

_____

_____

_____

According to Ephesians 3:20–21, what should be true of our expectations?

_____

_____

 Behind the Scenes

The biblical definition of faith in Hebrews 11:1 clearly leads us to understand that faith must far exceed humanism and avoid mere subjective, philosophical ideas. The concept of faith, according to God's Word, entails understanding that: 1) the entire creation, visible and invisible, is the result of a Creator's direct, intelligent action and not the product of blind chance (Hebrews 11:3); 2) historic figures have encountered this Creator in personal ways, evidencing He is more than merely a force—He is a personal God who relates in providential and redemptive ways to those who seek Him (Hebrews 11:2, 4–39); 3) any worthy approach to God, with true faith, must believe these two propositions if faith is to have a starting place and a realizable goal.

Probing the Depths

As you read through Hebrews, you encountered many whose lives are now held up as examples of power faith. These are people of whom God "is not ashamed to be called their God" (Hebrews 11:16). The obvious thought is that, sometimes, God *is* ashamed! When is that? Whenever our faith is an attempt to appropriate the goodness of God for this life only, forgetting that His plan is an eternal one!

The Bible is clear in its teaching concerning the power of faith. However, many believers are confused concerning matters of faith. This confusion exists in part because of the variety of high-profile "faith" ministries. Some minister effectively, while others appear to use faith in such a way that makes man the master of his own destiny, rather than God the Sovereign Lord. Any teaching that exalts the created over the Creator is in error. We must never fail to remember that "it is God who works in [us] both to will and to do for *His* good pleasure" (Philippians 2:13). God is in control of our lives; our faith is a gift from Him, not a means to manipulate the Almighty.

The faith litany found in Hebrews 11:13–16 can become a grid work for evaluating your faith life. Some think these verses contain a contradiction to understanding the life of faith: "These all died in faith, not having received the promises . . ." However, true faith remains intact whether we experience the circumstances of our victory or only receive it through strong, sure faith.

To live a life filled with power faith, we must understand that the practical purpose of our faith life is to bring us where God wants us to go. It is not a tool for self-accomplishment, but for God's accomplishing His purpose in us as we actively, aggressively open up to His Word, will, promise, and power.

 Kingdom Life—*Attributes of Faith*

In Hebrews 11:13–16, a remarkable litany of faith is recited. If you memorize this rhythmic statement of faith, your personal faith life will be greatly enhanced. Now note five more characteristics of faith these verses reveal:

1. *Faith is fully persuaded.* Paul uses this word when he says he has become persuaded that nothing can separate the believer from God's love in Christ (Romans 8:38–39). It always involves a process of thought; persuasion requires process and time. He uses the same word again to speak of the confidence he has in Christ finishing the good work He has begun in every believer (Philippians 1:6).

   Perhaps the most moving usage of this word occurs when Paul writes to Timothy, who has begun to battle fear as a pastor in Ephesus. As a loving father, he invites Timothy to take his place in the work of faith, saying, "I am not ashamed, for I know whom I have believed, and am *persuaded* that He is able to keep what I have committed to Him until that Day" (1 Timothy 1:12). The Greek used for *persuaded* is *peitho* (*Strong's #3982*). It has the meaning of having experienced a debate in which all the relevant ideas have been given a fair hearing—when all the issues have been considered, a decision is made based on all the evidence and an inner conviction. When this has happened, you are persuaded.

This persuasion comes by considering all God's Word has to say on the issues and by exposure to the person of the Word, the Lord Jesus. The combination of the written Word and the revealed Word in the person of Jesus Christ accomplishes this glorious persuasion. The question is: What "words" of promise form the basis for your current persuasion?

2. *Faith embraces.* This word (*aspadzomai, Strong's #782;* oss-pod'-zuh-my) is most often used in the beginning of the epistles when the writer "greets" the church. Sometimes the apostle will instruct the believers to greet one another—this is that word. It can mean to enfold someone in your arms, to salute (greet), or to welcome. As the assurance of faith involves considering the promises and becoming persuaded by them, so "embracing" means to take them in! Now that you see them for what they are, greet them, hug them, hold them, welcome them into your life. As you would embrace a loved one, so you are to treat the promises God has spoken into your life.

3. *Faith confesses.* The Greek word *homologeo* (*Strong's #3670;* hahm-ahl-ahg-eh'-oh) means to give assent, covenant, or to acknowledge. A contractual meaning is suggested, as when a building project is to begin. Jesus uses this word when He says, "Whoever confesses me before men, . . . [I] also will confess . . ." (Luke 12:8). It means to speak the same thing. Faith aligns the persuading word with the embraced word to the spoken word. What should you be confessing in your present circumstance? You should be confessing what you have become persuaded of—you should be confessing what you are welcoming

into your life. Put it in the negative: What should you not be confessing? You should not confess things of which you are not persuaded. You should not be confessing things you are, in fact, not welcoming into your life.

Jesus said, "Out of the abundance of the heart, the mouth speaks" (Matthew 12:34). God's Word reveals what is in God's heart; realize your words will reflect your own heart attitudes. The question is: What is the condition of your heart toward the promises of God as indicated by your confession?

4. *Faith declares plainly.* Why is this different from what we just studied? The preceding has to do with vocabulary—the words you have been using that tell the condition of your heart toward the promises of God. This present declaration comes more as a manifestation of a life decision you have made that is evident to all. The Greek word for manifest, *emphanidzo* (*Strong's #1718;* em-fan-id'-zoh), is used to describe the manifestation of life, what others can plainly see because of life-style and conversation. Jesus uses this word when speaking of the spiritual manifestation He and the Father will make to every believer when the Holy Spirit is received (John 14:21).

The combination of words used here in Hebrews (11:14) suggests clarity. There can be no disputing of what is being declared. It is obvious. The "plainly declaring" phrase may certainly involve language, but it is much more than that. If you are around someone who is "declaring plainly" (as the word is used here), you will hear what is being spoken through body language, decisions, actions, and their words. Their life "plainly declares." And in this instance, the lives of these believers "plainly declared" that they had become persuaded of God's promise, that they had welcomed God's promise into their lives, that they were speaking what God what was promising, and that their entire life-style proved that this faith was real. The question is: What is your life telling others about your faith?

5. *Faith calls to mind.* The idea here is more than just to remember. The concept is that of controlling your thought life; being in charge of what you are thinking. It also implies controlling your thoughts by speaking of the thing you wish to remember.

The apostle writing this letter teaches all who are serious about their faith a remarkable lesson: If you place in your mind an objective other than the one outlined in God's promise, you'll have an opportunity to reach that objective! Amazing, isn't it?

If the pilgrims of Hebrews 13:13 had focused on the country they left behind to follow God's call, numerous opportunities to go back would have appeared. Rather, they focused on the land of God's promise; a better, heavenly country. They "called to mind" a goal that rested in the center of God's promises.

The important thing to remember is that we are to be in absolute control of what we think. Though some may say this can be overdone, God would not give instructions on how to think (see Philippians 4:8) if it were not possible to do exactly what He has said!

6. *Faith desires.* The Greek word *oregamai* (*Strong's #3713*; or-eg'-om-ï) signifies an inner choice to reach for something, to stretch oneself out to an extreme position of vulnerability, as in saying, "This is what I want to do with my life." It's the word used in 1 Timothy when Paul says that it's a good thing to *desire* the office of a bishop. In its negative form, it's also the word used to describe someone coveting an object not yet possessed. In the positive, you would use this word in the phrase, "This is the desire of my life." Faith desires the fulfillment of what God has promised. The question is: What is the desire of your life?

Read Luke 21:19; Philippians 4:8–9; Psalm 119:11.

Questions:

In what way does your thought life affect your walk of faith?

Realizing that "possess" means "to acquire control of," and that your "soul" includes your *mind* and *feelings*, what deeper understanding regarding the walk of faith can you gain from Jesus' words?

✎ _____

_____

_____

What steps can you take to better control your thought life and more effectively walk in a strong, sure faith?

✎ _____

_____

_____

Record Your Thoughts

Since "faith is the substance of things hoped for, the evidence of things not seen," write out some of the things you are hoping for but do not yet see. As you do, let the Holy Spirit remind you of God's Word. Write those promises alongside the things you're hoping for, but not yet seeing.

✎ _____

_____

_____

ADDITIONAL OBSERVATIONS

SESSION TWO

The Gift of Faith

Kingdom Key—*Know the Sources of Faith*

1 Corinthians 12:4–11 There are diversities of gifts, but the same Spirit. There are differences of ministries, but the same Lord. And there are diversities of activities, but it is the same God who works all in all. But the manifestation of the Spirit is given to each one for the profit of all: for to one is given the word of wisdom through the Spirit, to another the word of knowledge through the same Spirit, to another faith by the same Spirit, to another gifts of healings by the same Spirit, to another the working of miracles, to another prophecy, to another discerning of spirits, to another different kinds of tongues, to another the interpretation of tongues. But one and the same Spirit works all these things, distributing to each one individually as He wills.

The common faith experience is a matter of choice. The believer chooses to believe what God has said in His Word. But now we're looking at this other work of God's Spirit, when faith functions as a "gift" because *He*—the Holy Spirit—has simply *given it* into a situation wherein a Christian becomes the instrument He has chosen to use in ministering this gift. This faith is the gift referred to in the passage above, "to another faith by the same Spirit."

The gift of faith is a unique form of faith that goes beyond natural faith and saving faith. It supernaturally trusts and does not doubt with reference to the specific matters involved.

Kingdom Life—*The Gifts of The Holy Spirit*

Spiritual gifts are portions of God's grace. They display the personal, powerful presence of the Holy Spirit and are given to every believer for the common good of the church. Though we vary in what seems to be each believer's dominant gifting from God's creative work in us, the Holy Spirit will give us whatever is needed to minister to distinct circumstances. He distributes these freely and readily in the moment of need in order to enable the believer's ministry in Jesus' name. Spiritual gifts are not badges of honor or signs of spiritual maturity. They are not earned. Our attitude concerning the gifts is to be willing, available, goodhearted friends of Jesus. We are to be compassionate friends of those in need, confident of God's promises and power gifts to serve such needs.

Word Wealth—*Faith*

Faith, *pistis* (pis'-tis); Strong's #4102: The word means persuasion, i.e. credence; moral conviction of religious truth, or the truthfulness of God. It carries the connotation of assurance, belief, believe, faith, fidelity.

Word Wealth—*Gift*

Gift, *charisma* (khar'-is'mah); Strong's #5486: A (divine) gratuity, i.e. deliverance (from danger or passion); a spiritual endowment or miraculous faculty; a free gift.

Kingdom Life—*Supernatural Faith*

The Apostle Paul operated in the gift of faith many times throughout his ministry. The occurrences of this supernatural faith can be recognized in Paul's unswerving confidence regardless of his situation. At times of seemingly impossible odds, Paul's faith seemed to be limitless. It was a faith borne of God, not by strength of a powerful human will to believe.

When we study it objectively, the *gift of faith* appears to function without external stimulus—not dictated by circumstance. Paul did not gather up his courage and place his faith in his own hopes; his faith was based on the internal, not external. It was supernatural, not natural. And it was based on what Paul understood the Lord to be saying, rather than anything being spoken by earthly authority or generated by human will or religious zeal.

Read Acts 27:6–44.

Questions:

When you are faced with a seemingly impossible situation, what are your typical thoughts, feelings, and actions?

✎ _____

_____

_____

_____

What seems to be Paul's attitude before, during, and following the storm at sea?

✎ _____

_____

_____

_____

What can you learn from Paul's reactions that you can apply to your own circumstances?

✎ _____

_____

_____

Kingdom Extra

People who fully follow the Lord are able to see the Lord in their circumstances. They are not ignorant of the challenges, not playing mind games, pretending to deny the reality of what is being faced—they are seeing the Lord above and beyond the problems!

The gift of faith, that supernatural working of the Holy Spirit, comes to those open to and desirous of being filled with that Spirit. Like all the other gifts, the gift of faith flows to those who are allowing the Holy Spirit to work in them. Even when no external influence can be found to justify absolute assurance of a highly improbable solution, the supernatural gift of faith remains confident, convinced, and unshakeable.

The gift of faith requires a realization of God's absolute control, His limitless love, and our own human state. It is necessary that we walk in the kingdom attitudes of humility and submission for the powerful gift of faith to flow in and through our lives.

Even Jesus, though 100% God and 100% man when He walked this earth, lived His life in a continual attitude of submission and humility. He limited His activity to what He saw and heard from the Father. As you read the Scripture portions below, consider the wondrous fact that these words were spoken by the King of kings and the Lord of lords—the One present at creation and the One who will usher in the end of time.

Read John 5:19; John 12:49–50; Numbers 13:17–33.

Questions:

To operate in the gift of faith, it is first necessary we hear from the Father. Is this an ability you currently possess? How can you acquire or increase this ability in your life?

✎_____

_____

_____

_____

What can you learn from the story about Caleb that can increase your ability to hear from the Lord and open yourself to supernatural faith?

✎_____

_____

_____

Word Wealth—*Able*

Able, *yakol* (yaw-kole'); Strong's #3201: To be able; to have power; having the capacity to prevail or succeed. This verb is used 200 times in the Old Testament. Generally, it is translated by such English words as "can," "could," or "be able"; in a few references, "prevail" (1 Kings 22:22; Esther 6:13); sometimes, "to have power." In Esther 8:6, it is translated as "endure": the compassionate queen asks, "How can I endure to see the evil that will come to my people?" In Numbers 13, Caleb uses the intensive repetition of *yakol*: "Let us go up . . . we are well able to overcome it."

Behind the Scenes

Dr. Roy Hicks, Sr., says of Caleb's confession, "Caleb saw the same giants and walled city as the other spies, but the ten spies brought back an 'evil report' of unbelief. Caleb's words declared a conviction—a "confession"—before all Israel: 'We are well able to overcome.'" He had surveyed the land, a reminder that faith is not blind. Faith does not deny the reality of difficulty; it declares the power of God in the face of the problem.

There is a message in the spirit of Caleb's response to those who rejected his faith-filled report. While today some people use their "confession" of faith to cultivate schism, or to separate in pride, Caleb stood his ground—in faith—but still moved in partnership and support. For the next forty years, he moved alongside many whose unbelief delayed his own experience of victory. Here is tenacious patience as well as faith! His eventual, actual possession of the land at a later date indicates that, even though delays come, faith's confession will ultimately bring victory to the believer.

Kingdom Life—*Faith Beyond Ability*

Begin this section by reading Acts 3:1–16.

Please note that the healing required a choice by Peter. He chose to extend his hand to the lame man and to pick him up. He chose to speak the healing words in the name of the Lord Jesus. But in responding to the amazement of everyone as they saw the lame man now walking, jumping, and praising God, Peter declared it was faith that healed him. And more important to our discussion, Peter also declared that this faith came "through Him (and) has given him this perfect soundness in the presence of you all."

Peter recognized the operation of this faith was not premeditated. This faith is not a function of character or personal acquisition. Though *obedient* choice is certainly involved, Peter made it clear that nothing of personal holiness, self-will, or personal power had accomplished this wonderful miracle (Acts 3:12).

Peter acknowledged that this miracle was made possible by a faith whose source is beyond human initiation. This supernatural faith can be and is to be cooperated with; it can be and is to be released through human agency. But above all, this faith "comes from Him!"

Read Romans 10:17; Hebrews 11:1, 6.

Questions:

How do the truths of these verses interact with or enable the gift of faith?

✎ _____

_____

_____

Has the realization of supernatural faith's characteristics altered your understanding of faith? In what way(s)?

✎ _____

_____

_____

What steps can you take to increase your ability to follow the Holy Spirit into areas wherein supernatural faith is required?

✎ _____

_____

Kingdom Extra

In this first recorded miracle performed by the disciples, we are given the key for use by all believers in exercising faith's authority. When commanding healing for the lame man, Peter employs the full name/title of our Lord: "Jesus Christ [Messiah] of Nazareth." "Jesus" ("Joshua" or "Yeshua") was a common name among the Jews. But the declaration of His full name and title, a noteworthy practice in Acts, seems a good and practical lesson for us (see Acts 2:22; 4:10). Let us be complete when claiming our authority over sickness, disease, or demons. In our confession of faith or proclamation of power, let us confess His deity and His lordship as "the Christ" ("Messiah"); use His precious name, as "Jesus" ("Savior"). Call upon Him as "Lord Jesus" or "Jesus Christ" or "Jesus of Nazareth." There is no legal or ritual demand intended in this point, but it is wise to remember, even as we pray "in Jesus' name" (John 16:24), so we exercise all authority in Him—by the privilege of power He has given us in His name (Matthew 28:18; Mark 16:12–20; John 14:13, 14). Many other compound names for Him are found in the Word of God. Let us declare them in faith, with prayer and full confidence.

Probing the Depths

This chapter on the "Gift of Faith" will be followed by the chapter, "The Choice of Faith." This is intentional. However, neither chapter is presented as an alternative. Some in the renewal movement within the church have become polarized on the question, "Is faith sovereign, or is faith all a matter of human choice?"

Two personalities from the early days of renewal illustrate the different positions: Charles Price and Smith Wigglesworth. Both were evangelists, Price from Canada and Wigglesworth from Great Britain.

Charles Price preached that all faith was a matter of the sovereignty of God. If you didn't have faith, there wasn't a thing you could do about it! Either you had it, or you didn't! Price said, "God will move, then you may follow." A story is told of the evangelist Price. A young man entered the church service late and was ushered to the front row. Though late, he noticed that the meeting hadn't yet started. He whispered to the man sitting next to him, "What, haven't we started? Where is the evangelist?" To his surprise, he heard, "Young man, I *am* the evangelist. But we are not starting until the Lord has arrived!"

Smith Wigglesworth believed quite differently. His message was, "*You* move, and then *God* will move!" He is famous for outlandish behavior. This story illustrates his position on matters of faith: He once pulled a woman from her wheelchair with the command, "Be healed!" Instead of being healed she fell down. Everyone else was quite embarrassed. Not Wigglesworth. He calmly put her back in the wheelchair and said, "Young woman, you fell because you tripped over your blankets." Again he pulled her from the wheelchair with the command to be healed. And she *was!*

Both men had extraordinary results in seeing many people healed, but their methodologies were quite different. Since both ministries occurred quite early in the renewal movement of this century, the church's understanding of faith and the miraculous was just beginning to be developed. Since then, many are tempted to, or actually do, polarize on the question of God's sovereignty vs. human participation. But when we're faced with the question today, "Is faith all God, or is faith all man?" the best answer is "both!" There is the *gift of faith* (from God, Who sovereignly gives), and there is the *choice of faith* (by man to actively receive).

Our faith life will be complete only if we will make room for both.

Record Your Thoughts

Write a personal experience you have had with the "gift of faith."

✎ _____

_____

_____

_____

_____

_____

What are those things you can do that make you responsive to the working of the Holy Spirit who brings the manifestation of the gift of faith?

✎ _____

_____

_____

Romans 12:3–8, says that you have received a "measure" of faith. Everyone has. Honestly evaluate how you are using the measure of faith you have been given.

✎ _____

_____

_____

ADDITIONAL OBSERVATIONS

SESSION THREE

The Choice of Faith

 Kingdom Key—*Decide to Believe*

Mark 4:35–41 . . . [Jesus] said to them, "Let us cross over to the other side." Now when they had left the multitude, they took Him along in the boat as He was . . . And a great windstorm arose, and the waves beat into the boat . . . But He was in the stern, asleep on a pillow. And they awoke Him and said to Him, "Teacher, do You not care that we are perishing?" Then He arose and rebuked the wind, and said to the sea, "Peace, be still!" And the wind ceased and there was a great calm. But He said to them, "Why are you so fearful? How is it that you have no faith?" And they feared exceedingly, and said to one another, "Who can this be, that even the wind and the sea obey Him!"

It is significant to note that Jesus rebuked both the storm and the disciples! Though He made the storm on the *outside* cease, He expected them to deal with the storm on the *inside*. As you read through the Gospel narratives, you will be surprised by how often Jesus will control the elements and control demonic spirits—yet you will hardly ever see Him controlling the disciples. Only *He* could rebuke the storm on the Sea of Galilee. Only *they* could rebuke the storm of fear and doubt they were experiencing.

When He asks, "Why is it that you have no faith?" he is suggesting that faith was possible—that it was a matter of choice. They could have chosen to believe instead of giving in to their doubts and fears.

This is true for us, too. In His wisdom, God has made us responsible in matters of faith. Only we can deal with doubts and fears. If Jesus says, "Fear not," it must be possible for us to receive that mastery over fear! He would not give us the admonition if we were incapable of following the directive.

Read Mark 5:35–36; James 1:6; Ephesians 6:10–18.

Questions:

What situations cause you to struggle with fear?

✎ _____

_____

_____

Are you aware of having made a decision to not operate in faith?

✎ _____

_____

_____

_____

What does this tell you about the necessity of making a decision to operate in faith?

✎ _____

_____

_____

In what way(s) does this understanding of faith help you grasp that faith is active, not passive?

✎ _____

_____

_____

 Word Wealth—*Fear*

Fear, *phobos* (fob'-oss); Strong's #5401: This Greek word means alarm or fright; to be afraid, exceeding fear, or terror. In Romans 8:15, Paul associates this terror with the spirit of bondage and writes that we have not been given that spirit.

We have received the working of the Holy Spirit that is called the "spirit of adoption." He will lead us to exclaim, "Abba Father", an endearing term used by those who know that they are included in the family of God and have no reason to fear.

Fear, *deilia* (di-lee'-ah); Strong's # 1167; This Greek word means timidity or fear. In 2 Timothy 1:7, Paul reminds Timothy that ". . . God has not given us a spirit of fear, but of power and of love and of a sound mind." In the last lesson, we considered faith as a gift of the Holy Spirit. When we consider faith as a choice, let us never think that we are left alone! God's Spirit is working into us the knowledge that each of us is a child of the Father. By this means, the Holy Spirit is seeking to give us power, love, and a sound mind.

 ## Kingdom Life—*Stand Strong*

The Greek word *sophronismos* (so-fron-is-mos'; Strong's #4995) is translated as "sound mind" in 2 Timothy 1:7. The Greek word conveys the idea of discipline, and self-control. While the word "fear" means timidity and a loss of confidence, "sound mind" refers to the ability to be under control during difficult circumstances, to think straight under pressure.

The bad news: there *is* a spirit of fear that will seek to overcome you during times of difficulty. The good news: the Holy Spirit makes a sound mind available to you at the same time.

You can choose to take your thoughts and feelings captive and stand strong, or you can choose to panic, giving in to doubts and fears. The choice is yours. Using the metaphor of the story in Mark 4, if the Lord Jesus says, "Let us go over to the other side," it is reasonable to assume you will make it!

The question then becomes, "What has the Lord said to you?" Or perhaps better said, "What Scriptures do you know which may be applied to your current set of circumstances?"

If some aspects of faith are a matter of choice, and, if the choice is between what you know the Lord has said and what your circumstances are saying—or what the enemy of your soul is saying—then knowing what the Lord is saying becomes extremely important!

Read 2 Corinthians 10:4–5; Philippians 4:6–8.

Questions:

In what ways does your thought life interfere with or disrupt your walk of faith?

_____

_____

_____

How does this fact relate to the amount of time you spend in God's Word?

_____

_____

_____

_____

 Behind the Scenes

Paul tells us in Romans 10:17: ". . . faith comes by hearing, and hearing by the word of God." From this we understand that, in God's ordinary means of operating, people do not come to saving faith unless they either read the Bible or have someone tell them the gospel message that is in it. It is the Word of God that the Spirit uses to awaken a response of faith within us, and it is the reliability of the Word of God on which we rest our faith for salvation.

Kingdom Life—*God is With You*

Where faith is a matter of choice, you can be confident that God's Spirit is speaking the Word upon which you may base your choice to believe. Again using the story of the storm from Mark 4, let us notice that the disciples had His word ("Let us go over to the other side"), and they also had His presence (He was with them in the boat)—He was with them!

He is also with you! Armed by what He has spoken to you, make good choices—choices to believe. Be responsible in dealing with your doubts and fears. Remember, Jesus will rebuke the storm on the *out*side. Only you can rebuke the storm on the *in*side.

It is not responsible or necessarily even truthful to say, "I am not afraid." But it is responsible to say, "I will not let fear win." It is not responsible to say, "I do not have any doubts." It is responsible to say, "I will not give in to doubts."

Read Matthew 28:20; Psalm 56:3–4; Isaiah 12:2; Psalm 92.

Questions:

What reasons can you find in these verses to choose faith rather than fear?

✎ _____

_____

_____

_____

What do you now understand to be the opposite of faith?

✎ _____

_____

_____

_____

Making the choice to believe is not the power behind faith. That power is the Lord alone. What role does our choice play in the victory of faith?

✎ _____

_____

_____

_____

Probing the Depths

The term "New Age" is one that has been around for quite some time. It has come to be a catch-all terminology for everything from recorded sounds of nature to ecology-minded movements. In actuality, New Age is a religion of sorts—actually it is a hybrid of all major religions, philosophies, and even draws from psychological and scientific teaching. It is a school of thought that teaches its proponents of a god who is merely a force and denies the existence of a Creator God who is intimately involved in the lives of His people. The New Age teaching claims many paths lead to God, denying that Jesus Christ, the only Son of God, is the only way to the Father.

Certain teachings about faith have been embraced by some in recent years. These teachings are more New Age than biblical. Let's look at the differences.

- New Age faith teaching leads you down the pathway of getting your way. Biblical faith teaching leads you down the path of getting God's way!
- New Age faith teaching makes your will important. Biblical faith teaching makes God's will supremely important.
- New Age faith teaching employs tactics of denial, refusing to acknowledge the reality of personal, supernatural evil. Biblical faith teaching acknowledges reality and triumphs through the tragedy.

Faith is never afraid of reality. Some people want to believe for healing because they are afraid of sickness. But biblical faith contends for healing because God has promised it ("I am the Lord who heals you"—Exodus 15:26), not because we fear the complications or implications of affliction or death.

This is not to suggest that a believer never fears, whether pain, sickness, poverty, or even the Enemy. Sincere, faithful believers experience fear of all these, but some adopt the art of denial, never admitting to fear, as though their denial is "faith." Genuine faith is centered in the Lord and His Word. It is based in Him—*the* Truth—and His Word which *is* truth (John 14:6; 17:7). Instead of living in a religious or philosophical world of denial, a biblical believer armed with faith's true understanding will refuse to be moved or to make decisions based on fear. That "true understanding" is (1) the Lord is with you, (2) His Word is true, and (3) He will not fail you or His Word.

Read Matthew 9:28; John 1:50; John 9:35; John 11:26.

Questions:

Why do you think Jesus asked in each of these cases, "Do you believe?"

_____

_____

Other than the question, "Do you believe," what similarities do you see in each of these situations?

_____

_____

What situations exist in your life that call for walking in faith? Which scriptural promises apply to these situations? Do you believe?

_____

_____

_____

Record Your Thoughts

In the previous lesson, you studied the *gift of faith*. God's Spirit can move powerfully in you so that faith is less a matter of *making* something happen and more a matter of *letting* something happen. Because it is a gift, you can only receive it. We each *can* respond to a gift being offered. We cannot initiate the offering of that gift, but we can receive it.

In this chapter, you have studied the concepts behind faith as a *choice*. Evaluate your recent decisions in matters of faith in the following circumstances: Note ways you now choose to operate in faith in each of these areas.

In your home:

✎ _____

_____

In your job:

✎ _____

_____

In your health:

✎ _____

_____

In your emotions:

✎ _____

_____

In your ministry:

✎ _____

_____

This is a splendid exercise, but look back at what you have written. If you have written choices that express your desires, and not His will (as revealed in His Word), then you will experience something less of faith's power than He intends. Go over the areas again, and write in a Bible verse that addresses your circumstance. Make that truth the basis for your faith, and let God into your circumstance by that choice. *You* needn't feel it's *your* task to create or beget the power to bring solutions. Yours is simply to choose *Him*. *He* has the power, and He has given you His promise!

SESSION FOUR

Faith and Healing

Isaiah 53:5 But He was wounded for our transgressions, He was bruised for our iniquities; the chastisement for our peace was upon Him, and by His stripes we are healed.

The dynamic ministry of Jesus not only revealed God's heart of love for mankind's need of a Redeemer, but unveiled God's compassionate heart of mercy for mankind's need of a Healer. The will of God was perfectly disclosed in His Son; we are to seek ways to fully convey that perfect revelation. Just as the Fall of man introduced sickness as a part of the curse, the Cross of Christ has opened a door to healing as part of salvation's provision. Healing encompasses God's power to restore broken hearts, broken homes, broken lives, and broken bodies. Suffering assumes a multiplicity of forms, but Christ's blood not only covers our sin with redemptive love; His stripes release a resource of healing at every dimension of our need.

Read Matthew 8:16–17.

Questions:

Have you ever experienced the gift of supernatural healing (in your life or in the life of someone you know)? If so, what were the circumstances?

✎ _____

_____

_____

In what areas of your life do you now desire God's healing touch?

✎ _____

_____

List the promises of Scripture upon which you can stand in faith
to receive.

✎ _____

_____

Kingdom Life—*Healing Provision*

God's loving, healing provision is rooted in the atoning work of the Son
of God upon the Cross, the power of God through the Holy Spirit's ministry,
and the character of God, which is committed to seeking human wholeness. Put
another way, by nature God is a healing God. In terms of power, there is nothing impossible with Him. And legally, the work of Christ on the Cross opens the
door for a Holy God to administer His healing mercies to a people who would
otherwise be unqualified to receive His healing touch.

Matthew 4:2–25 is the first New Testament record of Jesus healing physical afflictions and bringing deliverance to the demonically
tormented. Some argue that Jesus healed during His ministry only in
order to demonstrate His deity. However, it is clear through the study
of Jesus' teachings and ministry that He healed out of compassion for
the suffering multitudes. As we take a closer look at healing in the New
Testament, it will become ever more obvious that Jesus intended healing
to be part of the Christian mission of deliverance. His Great Commission
includes the promise: "They will lay hands on the sick, and they will
recover" (Mark 16:18). He extends this commission on the basis of His
Atonement, His compassion, and His promise of power to fulfill His
word.

Read Matthew 9:36–37, 14;14; 2 Chronicles 7:14; Psalm 6:2, 3; Psalm
41:4; Isaiah 57:17, 18; Jeremiah 3:22; Hosea 14:4; Isaiah 61:1; Jeremiah
30:17.

Questions:

What can you learn about Jesus' healing ministry from the Matthew passages?

_____

_____

_____

_____

According to the remainder of the Scripture references, what does the Lord say He will heal?

_____

_____

_____

_____

Kingdom Extra

Isaiah 53 clearly teaches that bodily healing is included in the atoning work of Christ, His suffering, and His Cross. The Hebrew words for 'griefs' (v. 4) specifically means physical affliction. This is verified in the fact that Matthew 8:17 says this Isaiah text is being exemplarily fulfilled in Jesus' healing people of human sickness and affliction.

Further, that the words 'borne' and 'carried' refer to Jesus' atoning work on the Cross is made clear by the fact that they are the same words used to describe Christ's bearing our sins (see v. 11; also 1 Peter 2:24). These texts unequivocally link the grounds of provision for both our salvation and our healing to the atoning work of Calvary. Neither is automatically appropriated however; for each provision—a soul's salvation or a person's temporal, physical healing—must be received by faith. Christ's work on the cross makes each possible: simple faith receives each as we choose.

Read Isaiah 53; Matthew 4:23–25, 12:14–17; Psalm 107:20.

Questions:

Based on these Scripture references, what is your understanding of healing as it applies to your walk of faith today?

✎ _____

_____

In what ways have the preceding thoughts on healing increased your faith to believe?

✎ _____

_____

 Word Wealth—*Griefs/Sorrows*

Griefs, *choliy* (khol-ee'); Strong's #2483: This Hebrew word means malady, anxiety, calamity:—disease, grief, sickness. Use a Bible concordance to look up this word to see how many times it is used to refer to physical sickness.

Sorrows, *makob* (mak-obe'); Strong's #4341: This word is often translated "sorrow," "grief," and seems to refer to emotional pain, while the preceding word seems to refer to physical pain. Use a concordance to see how the word is employed by various writers of the Old Testament.

 Kingdom Life—*Know God's Revealed Will*

When we read Mark 1:40–45, we cannot question whether healing is God's will. In this passage Jesus declares His willingness to heal the sick. The leper was certain that Jesus was *able* to heal him; he was not sure that it was His will. But Jesus' response settled that question: "I am willing; be cleansed."

Some insist that we must always preface our prayer for healing with, "If it is Your will." How can one have positive faith when one begins a request with an "if"? We do not pray for salvation with an "if." "If it is Your will" is more often an expression of fear—a proviso to "excuse God of blame" if our faith or His sovereign purposes do not bring healing. If His will is questioned, leave the issue to His sovereignty and remove it from your prayer.

At the same time, one cannot intentionally be living in violation of God's will and expect His promises will be fulfilled. Where biblical conditions for participation in God's processes are present, they must be met; but let us not avoid either God's readiness or God's remedies by reason of the question of His willingness.

Read Isaiah 58:8; Exodus 23:25; Deuteronomy 7:15; James 5:14, 15.

Questions:

What are the promises contained in these verses?

_____

_____

_____

What are the conditions which must be met for the promise of healing to be kept?

_____

_____

What steps can you take to ensure your prayers for healing will be heard and answered?

_____

_____

Behind the Scenes

If bodily healing is included in the Atonement, and Jesus has declared His willingness to heal, why is it that many sincere persons are not healed? This question is often asked as an earnest inquiry and other times as an unbelieving challenge. Let no one think we judge anyone as "less saved" if they either disbelieve in today's healing promise or if they believe in it but are not healed.

The truth of the promise is not based on whether it is believed or successfully received. We simply proclaim this truth and leave the results to God, just as we witness or preach of Christ's salvation and leave the resultant decision with Him.

Though this is by no means an exhaustive study, we put forth this list of insights that may aid you in your attempts to understand when healing doesn't come.

1. One of the most common reasons why those who are prayed for are not healed is failure to comply with the conditions (see Exodus 15:26). All God's promises are conditional. Read Psalm 1.

2. Disobedience is another common reason why healing and other blessings may be denied. For insight into this fact, read the story of Saul in 1 Samuel 15.

3. Some who pray for healing do not receive for lack of faith. The basic condition for bodily healing is "faith." Read these verses for greater understanding of this fact: Mark 11:24, Acts 6:8, Acts 14:8–10, James 1:6–7, James 5:14–16

4. Sometimes one's prayer is not answered immediately, because God is delaying the answer to teach a lesson. Something like this appears to lie behind the words of Paul to the Corinthians in 2 Corinthians 1:3–5.

5. James said, "You do not have because you do not ask." Sometimes, when we have a need, we *hope* that the Lord will fulfill the need, but we do not actually pray earnestly for the healing. Let us heed the wisdom and promise James declares: "The effective, fervent prayer of a righteous man avails much" (James 5:16).

6. Sometimes prayer for healing is not effectual because there is some unconfessed sin that we must resolve. The truth of this is contained in James 5:16: "Confess your trespasses to one another, and pray for one another, that you may be healed."

7. Prayer for healing may well go unanswered if we harbor unforgiveness in our hearts. Unforgiveness is a serious, sinful, heart matter that can deeply interfere with our relationship with God. Read Matthew 6:14–15.

8. Finally, God's providential oversight of our lives may be such that we will never understand why God's covenanted promises and provisions are not manifested in the way we have understood them. God's wise providence is above our full comprehension. We must let God be God!

Our faith may be weak or incomplete in some regards. We, in fact, may not be healed at times, which should never be viewed as reason for condemnation (Romans 8:1). Nevertheless, in all things, let us praise Him for His faithfulness and compassion. This is a great environment for healing to be realized and is consistent with the Scriptures, which reveal that Jesus is *willing* to heal.

 Kingdom Life—*In His Steps*

There is no greater stimulus for us to gain faith for healing than the ministry of Jesus. Hebrews 13:8 says, "Jesus Christ is the same yesterday, today, and forever." This Wonderful One who is the same today as when He ministered the marvelous and powerful healings recorded in the Gospels, invites you and me to trust Him for His healing touch!

The Lord's provision of healing continues and is to be continued not only **to** you, but **through** you to a needy world.
Read Matthew 12:10–13; Mark 2:1–12; Luke 4:38–43; John 4:47–54.

Questions:

What impresses you most about Jesus in these passages?

_____

_____

What aspects of these verses most speak to you about yourself?

_____

_____

_____

What impact do these insights have on your ability to believe for and/or receive healing from the Lord?

✎ _____

_____

_____

Behind the Scenes

One claim for a biblical "proof text" opposing the present-day miraculous works of God is in 1 Corinthians 13:10. Supposing to glorify the importance of the Scriptures, human ingenuity has proposed that "that which is perfect" is the Bible—and since it has been completed, thereby all miracles and signs the New Testament holds forth are "passed away" or occurring no longer.

The Word of God reveals something quite different: "that which is perfect" refers to the completion of God's purposes through and beyond the coming of the Lord Jesus Christ (Romans 8:18, 19). That is when all of God's fullest will for us will be realized.

Record Your Thoughts

Take the time to write out the promises for healing that have come alive to you during your study through this lesson.

✎ _____

_____

_____

What conditions must be met in order for your faith to move "under God's hand"—to become fully released to receive these promises?

✎ _____

_____

_____

SESSION FIVE

Faith For Miracles

 Kingdom Key—*Only Believe*

Mark 16:17–18 And these signs will follow those who believe: In My name they will cast out demons; they will speak with new tongues; they will take up serpents; and if they drink anything deadly, it will by no means hurt them; they will lay hands on the sick, and they will recover.

In the gospel of John, we learn that, on the night He was betrayed, Jesus promised to continue the ministry of the miraculous through the disciples: "Most assuredly, I say to you, he who believes in Me, the works that I do he will do also; and greater works than these he will do, because I go to My Father."

In both cases, the continuation of the miraculous is based on the condition of believing.

Read 1 Corinthians 12:5–11.

Questions:

How do you understand the "gift of miracles" at this time?

_____

_____

Have you ever heard of or experienced a circumstance that had no natural explanation? How did this impact your faith?

_____

_____

_____

Behind the Scenes

In this chapter, we will review miracles in the ministry of the Lord Jesus. In each miracle, you will find a specific mention of either faith, an act of believing, or an admonition to believe. Before commencing the study, here are three observations which might be helpful to you.

Observation One: *The miraculous has been an integral part of every era of God's revelation to His people.* The Scriptures are interwoven with records of physical miracles, spiritual visitations, signs, wonders, and miracles of every kind. There were seasons when the word of the Lord was rare; "the word of the Lord was rare in those days; there was no widespread revelation" (1 Samuel 3:1). This rarity (in some translations, the word "rare" is translated "precious" to denote "unusual") is brought about by the unbelieving or disobedient character of God's people; not by the character of God—as though He became stingy with His loving displays of power. Indeed, the One "with whom there is no variation or shadow of turning" (James 1:17) seems to be aggressive in displaying His power on behalf of those who will believe.

Observation Two: *Miracles are manifestations of God's glory, and are for His glory.* Regardless of the type of miracle, no matter what kind of "sign," it flows from the Lord to manifest the glory of the Lord; that is, the excellence of His love, grace, mightiness, and power. Every miracle is also *for* His glory, that *all* praise, *all* honor is to be given to Him, and *only* to Him when the miraculous occurs.

Observation Three: *The miraculous is always tied to God's eternal purpose.* While miracles which alleviate human need and suffering may, and often do occur, ultimately the miracle is not merely about the human condition, but is linked to God's divine agenda.

Miracles are not available to enable us to get what we want: They are for the purpose of God's will being accomplished. This doesn't mean God cares only for His *program* and not for *people.* Nothing could be further from the truth, because people *are* God's program. But we need to keep the focus on Him. He's the fountain of love and power, and also the only One with all wisdom and understanding. We need to trust *Him* and call on Him with *His* purpose being our highest concern.

Read Mark 16:17–20; 1 Peter 5:6–7.

Questions:

In considering the message of these two passages, how does each play into the flow of the miraculous?

✎ _____

_____

What could be the result of failure to recognize God's eternal purpose as the bedrock of the miraculous?

✎ _____

_____

 ## Kingdom Life—*To the Glory of God*

As you study this lesson, you will see how many times the Lord Jesus commends individuals for their faith. It is good for us to see Him do this, for it indicates His delight—God's pleasure—with people "believing" in a way that welcomes and allows Him to do what unbelief would otherwise hinder.

As faith develops, it accesses the grace of God for the miraculous. Yet whenever the miraculous is released, even though mankind benefits, it is always for God's glory. (Read Isaiah 42:8.)

Human nature inevitably worships the *human* agent through whom God's miracles might flow, and praises the one God uses to work a miracle, as well as the miracle itself, or artifacts associated with the miracle. The ancient church has venerated objects associated with past miracles, supposing that there is some efficacy in the object. This human tendency has a history, even in the Bible.

Aimee Semple McPherson, an evangelist of the 1930s, powerfully used by God in the ministry of the miraculous, had a biblical slogan engraved on her pulpit in Los Angeles. It read, "We would see Jesus" (John 12:21). She understood this imperative as one who regularly participated in the miraculous. Ms. McPherson grasped the powerful truth that the miraculous is a manifestation of God's glory and is always intended for His glory!

Read Numbers 21:4–9; 2 Kings 18:1–4.

Questions:

What actions of the Israelites caused glory to be denied the Lord?

_____

_____

Why was it necessary that the object be destroyed?

_____

_____

Word Wealth—*Miracle*

Miracle, *pala* (paw-law'); Strong's #6381: A Hebrew word meaning: to be marvelous, be extraordinary, be beyond one's power to do. It is based on the word *pele* (peh'-leh) that means a marvelous thing, a wonder; frequently expressing the extraordinary aspects of God's dealings with His people.

Miracle, *semeion* (say-mi'-on); Strong's #4592: A Greek word meaning: a sign, mark, or indication, especially of the supernatural. The miracles of God are a sign of His power and authority and an indication to the world of His power working in and through His people.

Kingdom Life—And Signs Will Follow

The New Testament miracles are essentially expressions of God's salvation and glory. Wherever Jesus went, the miraculous followed. Why did Jesus perform miracles? Jesus answered this question Himself. He declared His miracles were the fulfillment of the promises of the Messiah's kingdom as foretold by Isaiah. Jesus' miracles were signs of the presence of the kingdom of God.

Jesus also understood His miracles as evidences of the presence of the kingdom in His ministry (Matthew 11:2–5; 12:28). Every miracle story was a sign that God's salvation was present.

We gain a deeper understanding of Jesus in His miracles. He is Lord over nature (Mark 4:35–41) and death (Luke 8:41–56; John 11:1–44). He is the Suffering Servant who bears the infirmities of others (Matthew 8:16–17). He is the Messiah who was to come (Matthew 11:2–6). He fights the battle against evil (Mark 3:23–30; Luke 11:18–23).

Jesus did not work miracles to prove His deity or His messiahship. In fact, He clearly refused to work miracles as proofs (Matthew 12:38–42; Luke 11:29–32). His death and resurrection were proofs to Israel. to Israel. However, Jesus' miracles do give evidence that He was the Son of God, the Messiah.

God began His church with a powerful display of miracles (Acts 2:1–13). Miraculous powers were also present in the apostles (Acts 3:1–6, Acts 9:32–35, Acts 9:36–42). Ability to work miracles was taken as a sign for apostleship by Paul (Romans 15:18–19; 2 Corinthians 12:12). Thus, the ability to work miracles is not only an expression of God's salvation but also God's way of authenticating His apostles.

The lists of the gifts of the Spirit in the New Testament show miracles were one of the means by which believers ministered to others (Romans 12:6–8; 1 Corinthians 12:8–10, 28–30; Ephesians 4:11–12). This is sufficient evidence to verify that the working of miracles by the power of the Holy Spirit and to the glory of Jesus Christ is still intended in the church today and available for ministry through any believer the Spirit may choose to use.

Read Mark 2:1–12; Luke 7:1–10; Mark 5:24–34; Matthew 9:27–31; Matthew 14:23–33; Matthew 15:22–28; Mark 5:35–43; Luke 18:35–43; Mark 9:17–29; John 4:46–54; John 11:1–45.

Questions:

In reading through these accounts of the miraculous, what similarities do you find?

After considering the message of these verses, what do you understand to be the most important and powerful element in being used by God as an instrument of the miraculous or receiving the miraculous into your own life?

_____

_____

_____

_____

What can you learn from these passages that may allow you to more effectively be used as an instrument of God for the flow of the miraculous into the world? To be more receptive to the miraculous in your own life?

_____

_____

_____

_____

Kingdom Life—*Expect Greater Things*

A vital key to walking in the pathway of God's miracles is to stay available to the implications of Jesus' words:

"Most assuredly, I say to you, he who believes in Me, the works that I do he will do also; and greater works than these he will do, because I go to My Father. And whatever you ask in My name, that I will do, that the Father may be glorified in the Son. If you ask anything in My name, I will do it." (John 14:12–14)

Miracles are released and received by faith. They are useful for the presentation of the gospel. A miracle may solve a human dilemma or mend a human condition. Whenever a miracle occurs, all praise and honor should be given to the Lord who performed it.

Record Your Thoughts

Write out a miracle of God you have witnessed or experienced in a past season of your life—recent or distant. How did your faith align with or open the door to the miracle? How did you give the Lord glory and honor for this miracle? In light of your study, is there a prayer you would like to make to God concerning His miraculous grace and power and your own life and service to Him? Write it out.

✎ _____

_____

_____

_____

ADDITIONAL OBSERVATIONS

SESSION SIX

Faith and Suffering

2 Timothy 1:7 For God has not given us a spirit of fear, but of power and of love and of a sound mind.

Far too often, what we perceive as faith is actually motivated by fear. In more instances than we care to admit, we pursue powerful faith because we are afraid—afraid to be sick, afraid to be poor, afraid to be sad, afraid of disease. Fear can be a powerful motivator. But if we want to operate in real, power faith, we must own up to the fact that the Lord isn't the source of the spirit of fear.

The Scriptures reveal three major areas of life in which believers will suffer: persecution, dealing with fallen nature, and the results of living on a planet dominated by the curse of sin. In each of these dimensions of suffering, there is a special provision of grace that God offers—grace that can empower the believer to be *victorious* over and beyond the suffering rather than to be *victimized* by it. There is no biblical reason to believe that in any circumstance God intends for us as His children to be anything less than victorious overcomers.

Read Romans 8:31–39.

Questions:

Of the seventeen things listed here that cannot separate us from the love of God in Christ, which causes you most distress, real or imagined? Why do you believe this is so?

What comfort can you find in the fact that Jesus now makes intercession for you?

_____

_____

_____

_____

_____

Kingdom Life—*Endure and Persevere*

Read 2 Timothy 3:10–12.

When Paul wrote to Timothy, whom he had left at Ephesus to pastor the growing church, he summoned the young man to be strong in the face of persecution. Now, read the context: verse 3:12. We are reminded of the price that Paul had paid to preach the gospel. As he wrote Timothy, all of us are thereby and to this day taught that when the believers set their lives on a course of holy living, there will be resistance!

Second Timothy 3:12 is often used to warn believers of the persecution they will suffer when following Christ. However, Paul also says two things that are critical to our understanding and action when we face such suffering.

- *I endured them!* This is not the tone of a victim. Paul is not lamenting. He is being honest with the facts of persecution. He has not surrendered to the feelings of persecution! He drew on God's grace and prevailed!
- *The Lord delivered me from every one of them!* Paul's experience is a model for us. For every believer who encounters persecution the message is clear—if you suffer persecution for your faith and godly living, Jesus Himself will deliver you!

Read 2 Timothy 1:12; Galatians 5:11: Galatians 6:12; John 15:20; 1 Thessalonians 2:14, 15; Matthew 13:21; 1 Peter 4:15, 16.

Questions:

Paul says, ". . . all who desire to live godly in Christ Jesus will suffer persecution." What form does the enemy's persecution take in your life?

_____

_____

Do you find it difficult to continue an effective walk of faith when persecution arises? Why do you believe this is so?

_____

_____

Based on what we have learned thus far about power faith, what steps can you take to endure and persevere through persecution?

_____

_____

Word Wealth—*Persecute*

Persecute, *dioko* (dee-o'-ko); Strong's #1377: to pursue (literally or figuratively); by implication, to persecute; translated as ensue, follow (after), given to, suffer persecution, press forward. The word picture is of a relentless enemy's pursuit: someone who chases and will not give up.

Kingdom Life—*Overcome Temptation*

Read 1 Peter 2:11–17.

Peter writes to us as "pilgrims" of faith and encourages us to arm ourselves in our minds for the fight against sin. Though this passage is also connected to persecution, Peter's admonition deals most directly with the suffering we face essentially because we have chosen to live differently than we did before we came to Christ.

In this passage, Peter addresses the suffering we will face in dealing with our fallen human nature. It comes in two forms: interior and exterior. Times of temptation will come to us just as surely as the Enemy came to our Lord Jesus Christ (Luke 4:1–13). But even when we don't experience any external stimulus toward sin, we all still have a fallen nature that can taunt us—a "self-life" that is completely capable of assailing us, and at times even sounding just like the tempter!

Read James 1:12–15.

Questions:

What are the reasons believers face the suffering of temptation? How have these proven true in your own life?

✎ _____

_____

_____

What are the rewards promised those who overcome temptation? How can/do you experience this reward as a current reality?

✎ _____

_____

_____

 ## Word Wealth—*Temptation*

Temptation, *peirazo* (pi-rad'-zo); Strong's #3985: to test (objectively), i.e., endeavor, scrutinize, entice, discipline: translated as assay, examine, go about, prove, tempt, try.

 ## Kingdom Life—*Empowered to Prevail*

Read 1 Corinthians 10:13.

This three-fold, power-filled promise enables every believer to have confidence in dealing with temptation.

1. No temptation will ever come your way unless you will be able—if you *choose*—to deal with it properly. Your Lord will not allow you to face temptations which are beyond your abilities.
2. Your Lord will *always* provide a way of escape (Greek *ekbasis;* an exit, a way out). Whenever He permits you to be tested, He'll provide a way out!
3. God's design in making the exit available is not to promote our weakness, but to build our strength! The words ". . . that you may be able to bear it . . ." include the Greek word *dunamis* (*Dunamis* means energy, power, might, great force, great ability, strength. It is sometimes used to describe divine power over-coming all resistance.) You will be *empowered* to bear the test.

Read Hebrews 5:8; Hebrews 11:24, 25; Hebrews 12:1–4; Romans 8:16–18; Romans 8:26–28; Romans 12:21.

Questions:

What is to be learned from these verses about personal growth in the areas of suffering and temptation?

✎ _____

_____

_____

What is to be learned from these verses about victory over sin?

✎ _____

_____

_____

How can you most effectively put these insights into practice in your own life?

✎ _____

_____

_____

Probing the Depths

Some teach that a true believer should never experience sickness. But even though you are a true believer, regardless of how strong your faith may be, you are likely to encounter sickness.

We read in Philippians 2:26–30 the story of Epaphroditus. His sickness apparently came as a result of the ministry assignment he had received. People who are devoted to serving others and to Christ-exalting ministry still get sick. Though they are strong in personal faith and associated with those who regularly experience the miraculous (that would certainly be true of Paul!), God does not promise a life free of the trial of sickness.

We live on a fallen planet and are, therefore, exposed to the effects of the curse that include sickness, pain, and disease. But just as there is an answer for sin's temptation, there is also an answer for the effects of the fall that manifest as human sickness and affliction. Through the power of God, when we encounter sickness, His healing mercies are available to us.

It is a challenge to live in a fallen world. However, the believer who endures life on this suffering planet can lay hold of God's promises. Read Romans 8:18–28. It is clear from this passage that, as we deal with all the realities of sin's effects, the Spirit of God empowers us with our faith to live victoriously, overcoming in all we do, and extending that life of victory to everyone among whom the Lord has placed us.

Record Your Thoughts

Write out your personal philosophy for suffering in the three dimensions we have discussed:

1. Persecution:

2. Dealing with sin:

✎ _____

_____

_____

3. Life on a fallen planet:

✎ _____

_____

_____

Read Romans 8:19–22 and 1 Corinthians 4:11–13. A study of these verses can help us catch the attitude of the early church in dealing with the realities of a world stained with the curse of sin. Write out your thoughts, especially making a note of the "promise" that distills in your thoughts as you read these verses.

✎ _____

_____

_____

ADDITIONAL OBSERVATIONS

Saving Faith

Kingdom Key—*Faith Is In Christ*

Romans 10:8–9 The word is near you, in your mouth and in your heart (that is, the word of faith which we preach): that if you confess with your mouth the Lord Jesus and believe in your heart that God has raised Him from the dead, you will be saved.

It may seem strange to study "saving faith" in the context of power faith. It may be argued that "saving faith" has more to do with theology and doctrine, while power faith is more a matter of practical application. However, the basic faith exercised at our salvation is not different from that exercise of faith that accesses the power of God. Whatever your experience when you received Jesus Christ as your Savior and Lord, you first realized you *should* receive Him, and then you accepted that you *could*; it's the same kind of faith we have been talking about!

Saving faith is *faith in God through the person of Jesus Christ*. The focus of saving faith is always toward Jesus *personally*, not toward Jesus as a mere idea. In other words, the moment our study of God's Word becomes separated from Jesus Himself, it becomes only an academic pursuit without the power of the Spirit teaching us and glorifying Jesus in us through the Word. However true the Scriptures are, and however wonderful their wisdom is, the *life* of the Scriptures is linked to Christ. We dare not separate the Word from the Person.

Two things must be firmly established in our minds regarding faith: First, all vital matters center in the Person of Jesus Christ, not in things, ideas, or even faith in faith. This is what separates living faith from formula faith or mind-science systems of belief. Second, *saving faith is awakened through the word of the gospel*.

Read Acts 24:24; Galatians 3:26; Colossians 1:14, 2:5; John 1:12.

Questions:

What two responses are required of those who will be born again?

_____

_____

In recalling your own salvation experience, in what way did these two responses come into play?

_____

_____

At this point in our study, how do you see these responses as applicable to a walk of power faith?

_____

_____

Kingdom Life—*Experience the Miraculous*

If we belong to the Lord, we have all experienced the miraculous in our lives—*saving faith is miraculous.*

Our salvation isn't a miracle because we were especially evil before accepting Christ. We may or may not have been evil in the sense of being dedicated to the reprobate, depraved, or the terrible. But still, we were lost—without hope (Ephesians 2:12). Nothing we could do by any demonstration of human thought, strength, wisdom, or goodness in actions could rescue us.

But Jesus did. He rescued us! *Miraculously!*

It is the normal tendency of human nature to forget the absolutely, overwhelmingly miraculous nature of this provision and power operating at the time of our experience of saving faith. With the passing of time, too easily does our personal conversion become a memory of special times of long ago. However, if we can keep in view the miraculous nature of our "saving faith," we can keep prepared to experience ongoing power moments of faith operating in life's *daily* circumstances just as our salvation did at our life's *decision* point!

But if we forget the simple, yet miraculous, nature of our original "saving faith"—how God drew us unto Himself, how He persuaded us, awakened faith through the Word—we'll become insensitive to how He is ready to deal with us today, and will be unprepared or slow to respond in faith.

Quite literally, every area of your life is presently intended to experience the initiating, drawing, winning, persuading work of God through His Word and His Spirit. Miraculously, He is provoking us toward faith for ourselves, our marriage, our children, our business—every area of life.

Read Ephesians 2:8–9.

Questions:

What three forces do you see in motion in this passage?

✎ _____

_____

In what ways have these forces impacted your day-to-day life since you accepted Jesus as Savior and Lord?

✎ _____

_____

_____

 Kingdom Life—*Continue in Faith*

Read Romans 10:6–10.

In this passage is found the most foundational lesson in the importance and power of faith's confession. The principle is established at the very beginning of our life in Christ. Just as salvation (God's righteous working in our behalf) is appropriated by heart belief and spoken confession, so His continuing work in our lives is advanced by the same means. Our oral confession of faith declares, confirms, and seals belief in our hearts.

The word "confess" (Greek *homologeo*) has the connotation of a binding legal relationship established by and through declaration, as with a contract. Thus, as our words "contract" from *our* side the salvation God has fully provided from *His* by Christ's saving work and power, so we have a principle for all of life. Beginning in this spirit of saving faith, let us grow in active faith—believing in God's mighty power for all our needs, speaking with our lips what our hearts receive and believe of the many promises in His Word. Let us accept God's contracts for all our needs by endowing them with our confessed belief, just as when we were saved.

Thus the parallel between "saving" faith and "power" faith is seen in its dependence upon the Word of the gospel.

Read 2 Corinthians 4:13–14.

Questions:

In what way(s) do you see the relationship between God and those who have received His salvation through Christ as "contractual?"

_____

_____

_____

In what way does speaking forth our belief "seal" that belief?

_____

_____

Probing the Depths

Hebrews 12:1–2 says, "Therefore we also, since we are surrounded by so great a cloud of witnesses, let us lay aside every weight, and the sin which so easily ensnares *us*, and let us run with endurance the race that is set before us, looking unto Jesus, the author and finisher of our faith, who for the joy that was set before Him endured the cross, despising the shame, and has sat down at the right hand of the throne of God."

As you grow in your Christian experience, this facet of God's grace—that is, that He is the initiator, the Author of your faith—will not only become more precious to you, but you will also discover that this fact about our saving faith has the power to ignite our practical application of power faith in daily living. Since God is the initiator, the believer has only to discover what God is initiating; that is, what does God's Word say He wants to do? What is the Holy Spirit prompting you to accept? When we have discovered the provision God has already set in motion, we may confidently appropriate it in faith, just as we did at our conversion when we received Christ.

But that does not mean we will not experience obstacles or trials within our walk of faith. Life in this world will always include the temptation to sin and we will often be more inclined to trust more in what we see than in what we know to be true in God's kingdom. When weights or sin beset us, we must follow the example of our Savior—we must endure whatever comes, in order to receive what we have been promised.

Remember, "faith is the substance of things hoped for, the evidence of things not seen" (Hebrews 11:1).

 Kingdom Life—*Walk by Faith*

Read 1 Corinthians 2:9–12.

In this passage, Paul quotes from the prophet Isaiah. His intention is to show that the relationship we have with God through Christ is not something that can be appreciated with the natural senses. Not the eye, not the ear, nor even the heart can perceive the things which God has prepared for us.

Paul says that these wonderful things can be seen only as they are revealed to us by God's Spirit. His Spirit does not show these prepared things to your physical eyes, ears, or to your heart, the seat of human emotions. Rather, God's Spirit reveals them to your human spirit.

Verse eleven specifically says that it is in our redeemed human spirit that God's Word and revelation can be received apart from the distortion which comes via the eyes, the ears, and the heart.

These are simple lessons most believers learn early in their walk with Christ. However, though we may have learned the lessons long ago, *today's* dynamic faith life requires a review of those basic faith principles. Why? Because every promise we seek to apprehend will involve the test of our faith, and what Paul calls "the good fight of faith" (1 Timothy 6:12). Our faith will become strong only as we learn to trust His Word, walking beyond emotions—living and responding to circumstances by what we know to be true because of His Word, not by what we feel, see, or think on a natural plane.

True faith (saving faith or daily faith) does not rely upon nor respond to emotion and is not determined by what our senses reveal. It is based on the Word of God and activated by our precious Savior and Lord—the Author and Finisher of our faith.

Read Romans 4:13–25.

Questions:

What truth about the walk of faith contained in this passage most impacts you? Why?

✎_____

_____

_____

Abraham "contrary to hope, in hope believed." What does this mean to you?

✎_____

_____

_____

In what way did Abraham "endure" and what can you glean from his experience that can help you develop a strong, sure walk of faith?

✎_____

_____

_____

Record Your Thoughts

The faith you employ to trust God daily is that same faith you experienced when you first believed. Faith develops, faith grows stronger, faith evolves—*but it doesn't change its essence.* This is worthy and wonderful to observe and remember, because it points to how God is promising to meet every need in your life today—and to meet it through this same simple process of faith with which you began!

Write out your personal experience of saving faith. Describe how you came to believe in the Son of God. How did God draw you in? How did you first hear the gospel, the saving word of grace? As you write of your experience, ask the Lord to show you how He has continued His work of initiating the possibility for faith in your life. Ask the Lord to show you any corrections, any repentance you need to offer, which will correctively address your life of faith so it can once again become saving faith!

ADDITIONAL OBSERVATIONS

SESSION EIGHT

The Language of Faith

Kingdom Key—*Know True Faith*

Mark 11: 22–24 Have faith in God. For assuredly, I say to you, whoever says to this mountain, 'Be removed and be cast into the sea,' and does not doubt in his heart, but believes that those things he says will be done, he will have whatever he says. Therefore I say to you, whatever things you ask when you pray, believe that you receive them, and you will have them.

"From Jesus' own lips we receive the most direct and practical instruction concerning our exercise of faith. Consider three points:

1. Faith is to be 'in God'. Faith that speaks is first faith that seeks. The Almighty One is the source and grounds of our faith and being. Faith only flows *to* Him because of the faithfulness that flows *from* Him.

2. Faith is not a trick performed with our lips, but a spoken expression that springs from the conviction of our hearts. The idea that faith's confession is a 'formula' for getting things from God is unbiblical. But the fact that the faith that is in our hearts is to be spoken, and thereby becomes active and effective toward specific results, is taught here by the Lord Jesus.

3. Jesus' words 'whatever things' apply this principle to every aspect of our lives. The only restrictions are that our faith be 'in God' our living Father and in alignment with His will and Word; and that we 'believe'—not doubting in our hearts.

Thus, 'speaking to the mountain' is not a vain or superstitious exercise or indulgence in humanistic mind-science, but instead becomes an applied release of God's creative word of promise." (Dr. Roy Hicks, Sr.)

When it comes to the language of faith, every one of us needs a deep work of the Spirit, so that out of the abundance of our hearts, our mouths will speak words of faith.

Read Matthew 12:34; Proverbs 18:21.

Question:

In considering your conversation over the past few days, what strikes you about Jesus' words in Matthew?

✎ _____

_____

In what way do these passages bring you new insight or evoke questions in regard to the language of faith?

✎ _____

_____

At this point, what is your understanding of the importance of spoken words in regard to faith?

✎ _____

_____

 Probing the Depths

One of the grave dangers to the life of faith is legalism. Legalism is the attempt of man to reduce the grace of God to behavior not requiring the energizing work of God's Spirit. This is the same spirit of legalism that far too often parades itself as the definitive expression of a life of faith.

Within the church, there has arisen a movement based upon a repulsive new theology. According to this theological viewpoint, all should enjoy prosperity in this world. We hear, "Name it and claim it." We are told God wants us to prosper and enjoy wealth. We are told to visualize what we want, speak the word of faith, and then receive whatever we speak. This theology is only loosely based on Scripture. It is a distorted message based on a faulty understanding of a few passages which are twisted to promote the unbiblical proposition of wealth and prosperity for all who belong to the Lord.

However, it is only our luxuriant, American culture that can allow such a false teaching to breed. What do you suppose the impact of this teaching is on Christians in third world countries—those to whom a daily meal is a luxury? What does the all-should-be-prosperous message communicate to those who are homeless or suffer from debilitating, life-altering infirmity? What does this teaching speak to those who suffer dire poverty and want through no fault of their own?

We cannot reduce the grace of God to a formula. We cannot make demands on the Creator of all or attempt to control His behavior. These actions can point to more than legalistic expectations; they can, and often do, result in a sinful exaltation of self over the will of God.

We are not the first to face this kind of challenge to the true Gospel; wherever Paul preached, those who were called the "Judaizers" persecuted him. His gravest concern was that the new believers would fall into the trap of what he called "a different gospel" (Galatians 1:6–9). Without the warm, loving, vital power of the Holy Spirit, even the truth of faith's power when spoken *faith-fully,* can become "another gospel" sinking into the dregs of religious tradition.

 Kingdom Life—*Appropriate through Faith*

Jesus Himself established the importance of understanding how faith operates, when He said, "According to your faith let it be to you" (Matthew 9:29). Faith that believes is called to become faith that appropriates. The present day has seen a rise of understanding on this subject, but mixed with a confusing and distracting flurry of ideas that have often brought misunderstanding and criticism. Is there a biblically balanced approach to confessing God's Word in faith?

We must remember three major points regarding the language of and appropriation by faith:

1. The language of faith is not an attempt to create a false reality. Faith language does not deny any facet of the human fallen state—the earth's curse that has come upon mankind as a result

of original sin. It is not a "pretend" language, as though we could take ourselves out of poverty, sickness, divorce, or any other reality which we may see or experience.

But there is a way to respond to reality *in* faith. Instead of surrendering to the reality of the circumstance, faith will speak of what God's will is for the moment. Instead of dwelling on the reality's symptoms, faith will dwell upon God's promises. Instead of submitting to defeat or discouragement, faith will remember and praise God for His goodness.

Faith-talk does not practice the art of denial, but it *does* speak confidently of what God has promised to do within the reality we face.

2. The language of faith cannot be reduced to a matter of simply speaking positively. Negative attitudes and language can be shown to be the cause of many failures, but speaking *positively* is *not* the same as speaking *"faith."* The language of faith speaks God's Word, whether it is positive or negative! Faith-talk employs the promises of God, not just the good intentions of man. Positive speaking has plenty of value, but the language of faith accesses the throne of God. The language of positive speaking may move people, but it does not move the hand of God.

3. The language of faith CANNOT be practiced apart from the energizing work of the Holy Spirit. The Holy Spirit is the Spirit of *faith* and of *grace,* not "works." He gives living faith its dynamism. Nothing is shallower than the appearance of faith without its Holy Spirit-given substance.

Read Proverbs 6:2; 12:18; 13:3; 15:4; 16:24; 21:23.

Questions:

What observations can you make from these verses in regard to the power of speech?

What are some new insights you have gained or questions that have arisen?

✎ _____

_____

In what way does your life serve to prove or disprove the power of speech?

✎ _____

_____

How do you see this understanding as differing from the power of positive thinking?

✎ _____

_____

What other passages can you locate in Scripture that give further clarity to this topic?

✎ _____

_____

Word Wealth—*Power*

Power, *yad* (yawd); Strong's #3027: Old Testament word translated almost exclusively as "hand" as "into your hand," indicating power, means, resource, and direction. The graphic aspect of the Hebrew language pictures the tongue with a hand! The tongue can, as it were, "grab hold" of life and death (see Proverbs 18:21). The words you and I use have the power to grasp or release matters of life and death.

Kingdom Extra

Proverbs 16:24 reveals what God's wisdom (His Word) has taught our hearts: those truths and promises that are to influence our speech—to transmit that learning to our lips. The Word in our hearts is to teach or control our speech and conduct. The "sweetness" and "health" such speech promotes are desirable, whether in our human relationships or in the release of divine grace in our daily living. It leads the believer to an overcoming, victorious life, through a consistent acknowledgment of the power and might of God with both mouth and manner.

 ## Kingdom Life—*Do Not Presume*

Authentic faith is founded on the promises of God in His word; it is not presumptuous. Presumptuous ideas about faith lead to attitudinal or behavioral sin; and to missing the mark of faith's true meaning. Presumptuous attitudes are present when, in the name of "faith," a person either: 1) thinks faith is wishful thinking or a fanciful attitude, assuming God should relieve all their discomfort and jump to their request; or 2) rejects any responsibility on their part to offer a devoted heart and the commitment to serve Him regardless of their life condition. Presumption desires the promise *of* God without living a life *for* God and is hypocritical in His sight (Matthew 15:8).

To protect from a presumptuous attitude you must root your faith in what God in Christ has provided in His redemption, not on what you might gain through presumptuous faith exercises (Galatians 2:20). You must develop your own personal faith and do not attempt to live off another's faith (as did Sceva's sons in Acts 19:14–16). Walk in your own faith, growing in an intimate relationship with the Author and Finisher of your faith, so that you are known to be His and are found in Him.

Read Hebrews 12:2; John 10:27; Philippians 3:9 and Matthew 13:18 23; Ephesians 6:17, 5:26.

Questions:

What does it mean that Jesus is the "Author and Finisher of our faith?"

With these verses in mind, how do you now see the relationship between your faith and your words?

✎ _____

_____

How might you apply these verses to your life in a practical way?

✎ _____

_____

Are you willing to let God's Word become the pattern for your words? What affect might this have on your walk of faith?

✎ _____

_____

Word Wealth—*Confess*

Confess, *yadah* (yaw-daw'); Strong's #3034: In Solomon's prayer of dedication (2 Chronicles 6:24–31), he points to the importance of confessing the Lord's name (v. 24). The power-packed word "confess" opens a great truth concerning God's hearing and answering prayers. It is an appropriate word in Christian tradition, historically used to describe a position-in-faith or belief, as, for example, "The Augsburg Confessions." To confess belief is to say, "I openly receive God's promise and choose to take my stand here, humbly, *on* God's promises and in worship of His Person."

Yadah, the Hebrew word for "confess," contains and supports this idea. Derived from *yad,* meaning "an open or extended hand," the focus is on reaching to take hold of (see Word Wealth above). Just as a closed hand or fist may represent struggle or rebellion, an open hand indicates peace, submitted service or surrender. As Solomon comes with lifted, open hands, he comes in peaceful submission to God.

Yadah also involves worship, with open, extended hands, in a worship-filled confessing of God's faithfulness with thanksgiving and praise. This is the true spirit of the idea of "faith's confession of God's

Word": (1) to take a stand on what God says; (2) to speak what is believed with worship and praise; and (3) to do so in the humble spirit of faith in God's Person and promise. Such a stance will never be loveless or arrogant, and neither earth nor hell can successfully protest this confession of faith in heaven's power.

Kingdom Extra

Believing can take opposite forms. It can be faith or it can be doubt. When you believe that God exists and that He loves you and wants to meet your needs, then your believing creates faith in your heart.

Doubt is the reverse of faith, doubt tells you that God is not real or that He is unloving or uncaring about your needs. Doubt gives rise to fear, which brings torment, not peace. Fear actually keeps you from receiving the good things God desires to send your way. Do not shrink from expecting a miracle.

Expectancy opens your life to God and puts you in a position to receive salvation, joy, health, financial supply, or peace of mind—everything good your heart longs for, and more!

Pat Robertson, answering the question, "How do I pray for a miracle?" said this: "When we are faced with a great need for ourselves, or for others, we should begin by humbly seeking to know God's will in the matter: 'Father, what do You want to do in this situation?' Jesus said, 'My Father has been working until now, and I have been working' (John 5:17). He listened to the voice of the Father, and He watched Him. Be careful not to start or end a prayer by saying blindly, 'If it be Your will.' Rather you should seek to *know* God's will in the situation and then base your prayer upon it. Praying for a miracle is welcoming a gift of the Holy Spirit to manifest. When His will is to work one, He will witness this to your heart. Then you can ask Him to perform the miracle that you know He wants to bring about.

"It is often important to exercise a key to the miraculous—the spoken word. God has given us authority over disease, demons, sickness, storms, and finances (Matthew 10:1; Luke 10:19). Often, we may keep asking God to act, when, in fact, He calls us to employ His authority by our action with divinely empowered speech. Then we may declare that authority in Jesus' name: we may command needed funds to come to us, command a storm to be stilled, command a demon to come out, command any affliction to leave, command a sickness to depart.

"Jesus said, 'Whoever says to this mountain, 'Be removed and be cast into the sea,' and does not doubt in his heart, but believes that those things he says will be done, he will have whatever he says' (Mark 11:23). Believe in your heart that it has already happened! With the anointing of faith that God gives you, speak it forth. But remember, miracles come by faith in God's present power, not by a ritual or formula of human works or willpower."

Record Your Thoughts

Ultimately, your faith language depends on knowing the same thing that Paul knew. *It is the life of the Lord Jesus that makes sense of faith's confession.* Remember what Solomon said, "Death and life are in the power of the tongue" (Proverbs 18:21). Because we know Jesus Christ is alive, and, as the Resurrected One, He is ready to administer His mighty life-giving power to us—*now!*—in all of our present circumstances, we can choose to speak from the vantage point of life, not death. Our words of faith can confidently welcome and cooperate with God's will, as He has revealed it in His Word. We can enjoy the fruit of this language of faith—today and everyday—until Jesus comes again!

As a way of sealing this teaching in your heart and mind, write out a faith confession that has come to you during your study of God's Word on this topic. Also, write out a correction of something you have been allowing as an unbiblical confession that is inappropriate to your life of faith, and to your God-given potential use of the language of faith.

ADDITIONAL OBSERVATIONS

SESSION NINE

Faith and Restoration

 Kingdom Key—*Jesus Has Overcome*

John 16:33 These things I have spoken to you, that in Me you may have peace. In the world you will have tribulation; but be of good cheer, I have overcome the world.

Restoration implies that something has been lost. No one can live on a fallen planet, deal with personal fallen nature, and face fallen nature in the lives of others, without suffering loss. Learning to walk in faith will help you avoid many losses in life, but loss will still happen. When it does, because you have committed yourself to His agenda, you will experience the gracious and powerful restoring ministries of your God!

Read 1 John 5:4–5; Romans 5:1–4; Romans 8:37–39; Revelation 3:12.

Questions:

According to these passages, what allows us to overcome the trials and losses of this life?

_____

_____

When have you experienced loss in your life? What was your reaction?

_____

_____

_____

How might the truth contained in these verses have enabled you to walk through loss with greater ease?

✎ _____

_____

_____

Kingdom Life—*Expect Restoration*

In this lesson, you will study (1) God's restoration promises and program of which we have historical record; (2) the biblical concepts of restoration; and (3) God's restoration promises for your life.

Before we continue, we must face an issue that is an unfortunate and unhealthy aspect of our human condition. It is sad but true that it is in our nature to study faith so we can accomplish our personal agenda. It is an especially grievous situation when faith is sought out only for the meeting of personal need.

We must find a place of balance and truth in which to stand. On the one hand, God wants to meet all of our needs (Matthew 6:33). On the other, God is actually up to something! From eternity, God has committed Himself to a course of action from which He has never swerved. In executing that eternal plan, He graciously meets our needs. But the plan is much more than merely relieving the human condition.

Faith is at its best when we cooperate with God's eternal plan and join Him in His quest, instead of requiring Him to join us in ours! As we join in God's eternal purpose, we discover our needs being met while en route with Him to a final glory in which we have been included.

Read Matthew 6:31–33.

Questions:

What other verses can you locate that give voice to this truth?

✎ _____

_____

_____

When have you experienced God's provision or restoration as you simply walked the path He placed before you?

✎ _____

_____

_____

_____

What heart attitude is at the center of faith for the sake of receiving from God?

✎ _____

_____

_____

_____

What heart attitude is at the center of the faith described in Matthew 6:31–33?

✎ _____

_____

_____

_____

Behind the Scenes

Before we delve into the subject of God's restoration, let us look at an historical example of God's restoring power. To prepare for this and the following sections, take some time to read the books of Haggai, Ezra, and Zechariah. Each of these is fairly short, but the content is interrelated; reading them will prepare you to better grasp God's restorative nature.

Haggai and Zechariah were two prophets belonging to the Restoration Period of Israel. Israel had been destroyed and its people killed, taken captive, or exiled. Israel was then repopulated by the

Babylonians, and later the Persian Empire. Even before the deportation began, after years of humiliating defeats at the hands of the Assyrians, God spoke through His prophets, indicating that Israel would be restored to her lands. As the Restoration began to occur just as God had promised, Haggai was used to remind the people of God's plan.

Haggai prophesied during the efforts of Ezra and the people to rebuild Solomon's temple that had been demolished by the Babylonians. The date of Haggai's ministry was approximately 520 b.c. and is recorded in the Old Testament book bearing his name. Take some time now to read Ezra and Haggai.

The people of Israel had been living in exile following the destruction of Jerusalem by the Babylonians. They had returned and begun to rebuild, focusing first and foremost on the rebuilding of the temple. However, the people of Israel faced a herculean task and soon found themselves overwhelmed by three problems common to all people: disinterest, discouragement, and dissatisfaction. These three attitudes threatened to rob the returning Israelites of the restoration of their homeland.

God spoke clearly to Israel to wake them from their disinterest and apathy. He told them they were fruitless because they had turned from God's house. The people of Israel needed to come to the understanding that their own efforts could never produce lasting results. God would be glorified when they chose to yield to Him.

God also addressed the discouragement that overtook Israel. The older Israelites remembered the glory of Solomon's temple before its destruction by Babylon. They despaired of ever being able to recreate it and soon gave in to discouragement. God sent them another clear message: "be strong . . . be strong . . . be strong . . . and work" (Haggai 2:4).

The final issue God addressed in this story is dissatisfaction. The Israelites grew impatient and wanted an immediate restoration of all they had lost. After sixteen years of inactivity, they wanted an instant reversal to be magically visited upon them. The priests answered this expectation by reminding the people that uncleanness is contagious, but holiness is not. The application should be obvious: Do not expect three months worth of activity to undo the neglect of sixteen years. The word God spoke to the people was unexpected but eagerly received: '*But* from this day I will bless you' (Haggai 2:19). The people needed to understand that God's blessings cannot be earned, but come as gracious gifts from a giving God.

Kingdom Extra

In Ezra 1:7–11, there is a curious noting of certain temple artifacts. King Cyrus of Persia had ordered that these instruments which had been taken from Solomon's temple before its destruction should then be returned with Ezra. The verses even count out the number of knives!

Why is this partial inventory included in scripture? Read Jeremiah 27:21, 22. Approximately seventy years before, God made a restoration promise concerning the articles of the temple. "I will bring them up and restore them to this place." Why is this important? It indicates that whatever has been consecrated unto the Lord as His possession *remains* His possession!

You may rest assured that whatever you have consecrated unto the Lord—your life, your children—He treats as His and He will see to it that they are brought back!

Read Joel 2:25–27.

Questions:

What is your understanding of "the years that the swarming locust has eaten?"

_____

_____

_____

What things in your life have been seemingly "eaten" that you hope to see restored?

_____

_____

_____

Kingdom Life—*Be Faithful*

Zechariah's prophetic ministry addresses the same people but a different construction project. While Haggai's focus was on the temple, Zechariah's assignment had to do with the rebuilding of the walls and gates of Jerusalem. As the Book of Ezra gives the historical background for Haggai's prophetic ministry, the Book of Nehemiah does the same for Zechariah's prophecies. (You may wish to read the Book of Nehemiah at this time.)

The layout of the Book of Zechariah differs vastly from what you have just reviewed in Haggai. It contains a series of visions, their presentation to the people, and accompanying words of prophecy.

However, an overriding message is presented by both prophets: faithfully execute the call of the Lord in your life and complete the task He has assigned. This entails repentance for past neglect and renewed fervor for the task at hand.

Read Zechariah 4:6–10. As you answer the following questions, consider their application to your own walk of faith.

Questions:

What will *not* bring about restoration or the rebuilding of the city walls?

_____

_____

What *will* bring about restoration?

_____

_____

What will happen to the mountain, the obstacle which seeks to prevent the restoration?

_____

_____

When the final stone, the capstone (which many think is something called the "amen stone," the stone that locks the arch into place!), is placed, what is being shouted? What does this mean to you?

_____

_____

_____

Word Wealth—*Might*

Might, *chayil* (cha'yeel); Strong's #2428: As in Zechariah 4:6, this is an Old Testament word understood as "wealth," "valor" (courage), "virtue" (character), "an army." The issue here is dependence. What empowers your faith for the restoration you desire? As important as human resources are in the program of restoration, you must not allow yourself to depend on human ability, courage, sheer numbers, or force. Ultimately, true restoration is impossible without God! The word *power* is almost exclusively a strength word and is translated so. As the Hebrew prophets and poets often do, this coupling of might and power is a literary and polemic tool. The one word is built upon by the other, so that when combined, a fuller picture can be seen. Here, the prophet insists that restoration is impossible by human might and power!

Word Wealth—*Restitution*

To make restitution, *shalam* (shaw-lam'); Strong's #7999: Old Testament term with the figurative meaning: to be or to make completed; by implication: to be friendly; by extension: to reciprocate (in various applications). Translated as "make amends," "finish," "full," "make good," "repay," "make restitution." It has the idea of returning something to its rightful owner, or making amends, in the sense of attempting to put things back the way they were.

To restore, *shuwb* (shoob); Strong's #7725: To turn back (hence, away) literally or figuratively (not necessarily with the idea of return to the starting point). This word carries the notion of a fresh beginning. Going back to the start may be impossible in terms of time or geography. However, "restore" in this sense makes it possible to begin again.

Kingdom Life—*He Makes All Things New*

The concept of biblical restoration begins with the Law. As an example, read Exodus 22. The first several verses deal with restoring something stolen, and the making of restitution.

If the Law calls for restitution that replaces with more than what was lost, it is logical to assume that the Lord who authored that law would do the same! This is exactly what you read in your study of His restoration of the temple: He said that the glory of the latter house would be greater than the former. When He restores, He does something that makes the restored of higher quality than what was lost. In Zechariah 4:10, did you notice that the prophecy appears to rebuke the people for thinking that the rebuilt walls were to be despised as small?

The goal of this chapter is to provoke your thinking by reviewing some of the historical illustrations of God's willingness to restore, and His methods to accomplish restoration.

Read Job 42:10–12; Isaiah 42:22.

Questions:

What comfort and encouragement can you draw from the passage from Job?

✎ _____

_____

_____

Often, difficulty and loss create a "victim mentality" in the one who suffers. According to the verse from Isaiah, what is the result of this victim mentality? How can this attitude interfere with God's desire to restore?

✎ _____

_____

_____

Which of these passages most accurately reflects your attitude when experiencing loss?

✎ _____

_____

_____

What steps can you take to more closely mirror the attitude of Job?

✎ _____

_____

Many reading this study guide are asking restoration questions: "How can I believe for my marriage to be restored?" or, "How can I believe for my emotions to be restored?"

Ultimately, restoration is possible only when you believe it's possible. Believing in the possibility of restoration is provoked by the Word of God—the *rhema* (which means an utterance, or spoken word) of God. This is the Word spoken of in Isaiah 55:11: "So shall My word be that goes forth from My mouth; it shall not return to Me void, but it shall accomplish what I please, and it shall prosper in the thing for which I sent it." When you have a promise from God, you have the strength of God to bring that promise to pass.

Some might ask, "Is there anything that cannot be restored?" In response, let us review these passages of Scripture.

Read Psalm 51:10–12; Psalm 103:5; Isaiah 1:26; Isaiah 40:31; Isaiah 57:18; Jeremiah 30:17; Joel 2:25.

Questions:

As you review these passages, make a list of the things to which restoration is promised. Are any aspects of life not covered in these promises?

✎ _____

_____

What conditions are at work in receiving these promises?

_____

_____

_____

How do these promises apply to your own condition of trial or loss?

_____

_____

_____

Record Your Thoughts

Restoration is an active force in the lives of those in God's kingdom. We have His promises on which to rely, we need only engage our faith and learn to rise above the circumstances of this world. Now that you have begun your study on Faith and Restoration, write out what you are trusting God to restore in your life and in the lives of those you love.

_____

_____

_____

Session Ten

Faith and Prosperity

Kingdom Key—*Know True Prosperity*

Psalm 1:1–3 Blessed *is* the man who walks not in the counsel of the ungodly, nor stands in the path of sinners, nor sits in the seat of the scornful; but his delight *is* in the law of the Lord, and in His law he meditates day and night. He shall be like a tree planted by the rivers of water that brings forth its fruit in its season, whose leaf also shall not wither; and whatever he does shall prosper.

". . . whatever he does shall prosper." This includes everything: family, children, marriage, business, ministry, job, health—whatever you do! God intends what He says: *everything shall prosper.*

However, no promise of God is without responsible action to be taken on our part. No one will prosper until he starts doing what God says. We cannot leave out the first verses of this passage from Psalms; we cannot expect the result without the responsibility. Many people want the promise without the commitment. But none of us will ever gain anything truly worthwhile instantly and without effort.

The truly worthwhile takes time to develop. Do not expect God's answers to leap to *your* schedule. Remember, His answers occur when you first put His Word into action. Just as a period of intensive study precedes a college degree, so through patient pursuit of His promise let us wait for the word of God to mature in our lives.

Read Joshua 1:8; Proverbs 10:4; Proverbs 28:20; Matthew 6:25–34.

Questions:

Prosperity has come to be understood as financial security. However, *true* prosperity is so much more. What do you perceive to be true prosperity?

✎ _____

_____

_____

What is your current understanding of God's desire to see His children prosper? How do we position ourselves to receive this prosperity?

✎ _____

_____

_____

According to these passages and the Kingdom Key verses, what is the major prerequisite to receiving prosperity?

✎ _____

_____

_____

 ## Kingdom Life—*Be a Conduit for God's Blessing*

To secure a healthy perspective on this sometimes distorted subject of faith and prosperity, let's establish three conditions for prosperity.

Some of God's promises of blessing appear to have little restriction. Others are very focused, with definite parameters. But above all, it cannot be denied that we serve a generous God! It is in His very character to be liberal with His children. We must never forget, however, that one reason God blesses His children is for them to be a blessing to others. The conditions for blessing and prosperity almost always lead the believer down the pathway of *relationships.*

1. Prosperity is always linked to **purpose.** God intends for us to be instruments of resource. Read Philippians 4:19: "And my God shall supply all your need according to His riches in glory by Christ Jesus." When reading this promise in its context, the connection between the Philippians' responsible actions of giving

and the purpose of God's blessing is clear. They had given to Paul, and now God was rewarding them. But He was rewarding them so they could continue to be a resource for God's kingdom agenda.

2. Blessing is always connected to issues of **character,** God's and yours. Read Philippians 4:11–13. Almost in the same breath as Paul conveys the promise of blessings to those who have given, he is also administering the lessons of contentment. *Prosperity is never promised as a medicine for discontent.* Paul's confession is simple: I am content with or without. Possessions or prosperity are never to determine our contentment. This character issue is resolved by what one possesses on the inside, not on the outside. It is in the midst of this point that Paul makes this famous statement, "I can do all things through Christ who strengthens me." It is clear from the context that this strength from the Lord Jesus of which Paul boasts has to do with contentment in spite of the presence or absence of abundance!

3. Success has more to do with God's **agenda** than with our **desires.** It is *never wrong* for us to present our petitions—our desires—before the Lord. It *is wrong* to make our desires a condition of our relationship. God wants to bless us, to grant us good success in every area of our lives. But we will discover that those blessings come more quickly to those who are committed to God's agenda for their life.

The Bible contains both *promises for* prosperity and *warnings about* prosperity! Why? Because the Lord knows our hearts. Fallen man—even the Lord's redeemed—is easily trapped into patterns of thought regarding prosperity that lean toward greed. The Lord intends prosperity to be a blessing, not a curse. But when greed is the motive, when prosperity becomes the condition upon which our faith is based, our faith becomes misdirected. We find ourselves trusting Him **for** things, instead of simply trusting Him **in** all things.

Word Wealth—*Prosper/Prosperous*

Prosper, *euodoo* (yoo-od-o'-o); Strong's #2137: As used in 3 John 1:2 ("Beloved, I pray that you may prosper in all things and be in health, just as your soul prospers."), this word comes from the Greek words for "good" and "road." Thus it denotes success in reaching a goal, as in travel or in business.

John makes sure that the concept of prosperity is holistic. He ties together the condition of the inner person to the outer affairs of life. It would be unthinkable in his view to pray that you would get where you're going without being right on the inside. This prayer might be rephrased, "I pray that you will get where you want to go on the *outside* as long as you are getting where God wants you to go on the *inside!*"

Prosperous, *tsalach* (tsaw-lakh'); Strong's #6743: As used in Joshua 1:8 ("This Book of the Law shall not depart from your mouth, but you shall meditate on it day and night, that you may observe to do according to all that is written in it. For then you will make your way prosperous, and then you will have good success."), this Old Testament word means to push forward, in various senses; to break out, go over, be profitable.

These words spoken to Joshua as he was about to lead the children of Israel into the Promised Land underline the importance of God's Word in matters of faith and prosperity. *Tsalach* (prosperous) also carries the connotation of force. In fact, this word is often associated in the Old Testament with the coming upon a person of the Spirit of the Lord (see Judges 14:6 and 19 regarding Samson). In order for the new land to be occupied, there would have to be a breaking forth of God's power to assist Joshua. The word sometimes translated "prosper" is also used to describe how the Lord came mightily upon Samson during several of his mighty deeds of strength. It is as though the Lord were saying to Joshua, "I will come upon you and this people mightily for the taking of this Land, if . . ." Then, immediately following, this display of power associated with prosperity was conditioned upon speaking, meditating, and observing God's Law or the Word of the Lord.

Kingdom Life—*Prosperity Depends on Faith*

Can you see the connection between the conditions for prosperity and faith? Does it make sense to you that not one of these conditions for prosperity is possible without faith? Joshua could not have led Israel into the Promised Land without a strong, sure faith. Joshua's faith was emboldened by feeding on, thinking on, and constantly speaking forth God's Word of truth.

It is faith, in these expressions of speech, thought, and action, centered in God's Word, that becomes the basis for God-given prosperity. Remember the definition of the word: prosperity—getting to a desired place (See Word Wealth above.). The idea focuses less on material abundance than it does on successful ventures. Godly prosperity is the heavenly provision which makes it possible for us to advance successfully on our assigned journey or task to be accomplished in His will.

With these thoughts, let's also remember how the concept of force is associated with prosperity; it is a display of God's power and authority, never originating from human strength. I emphasize here: there *will* be resistance to your realizing God's prosperity. But God's power can overcome it and enable you to get where God wants you to go!

Write out your own thoughts as you study these verses dealing with the concepts of prosperity. Use a concordance to see what word is being translated as "prosperity," "prosperous," or "blessing." If there is an obvious condition which must be met in order for the promised prosperity to ensue, make a note of it.

Read Deuteronomy 29:9; 1 Kings 2:3; 2 Chronicles 20:20–22; 2 Chronicles 24:20; 2 Chronicles 26:5; Proverbs 28:13; Isaiah 55:11.

Questions:

What conditions to prosperity do you find in these passages?

✎ _____

_____

_____

What actions of the faithful in these passages enabled the flow of prosperity in their lives?

✎ _____

_____

_____

What is the overriding message you glean from these passages?

✎ _____

_____

_____

What steps can you take to place yourself into the flow of God's blessing and prosperity?

✎ _____

_____

_____

 Probing the Depths

Many people are handicapped by their own overriding life poverty, and too often their poverty is caused by their own disobedience to the Word. There are many ways in which people are disobedient; one way is in robbing God! Those who withhold their tithes and offerings are doing just that. As a consequence, they are robbing themselves of the blessings that God wants to bestow upon them. You see, when you do not tithe, you are breaking God's law; and if you are breaking the law, then the benevolent law of God cannot work on your behalf.

While we are most definitely living in the age of grace and Jesus fulfilled the law on our behalf, we are still responsible to live our lives based on God's will as revealed in His Word. There are principles in effect through the law that we engage by our obedience. One of these principles is found in the responsibility to tithe into God's "storehouse."

Nothing will keep a wise believer from tithing and giving, but he or she will never be found to tithe or give offerings just to get something in return. Rather, the act rises from obedience, and God *always* rewards obedience!

Read Malachi 3:10.

Questions:

What are your thoughts regarding the law of tithing?

_____

_____

_____

Do you believe tithing is required of the New Testament church? Why or why not?

_____

_____

_____

Kingdom Life—*Depend on God*

Biblical prosperity is impossible without learning to depend totally upon God, and unlearning the skills of depending on self. Prosperity can happen only when God alone becomes the believer's resource. Only then is it possible for us to avoid the poverty traps. The bank is not our resource; the government is not our resource; your monthly paycheck is not your resource. Most of the spiritual tests brought to the disciple's life focus on this key issue. Learning to look beyond the circumstances—to trust wholly in the One Who has promised to be your resource—is critical.

Ephesians 3:20 says, "Now to Him who is able to do exceedingly abundantly above all that we ask or think, according to the power that works in us . . ." God can and will provide far beyond our expectations; sometimes, beyond our imaginings. However, the word "exceedingly" does not mean excessively. Let us expect and contend for God's blessings upon our lives. Know that His generosity will exceed our norms, yet not lead us to ostentation or lavish display. His blessing is designed to focus people on the Blesser, not the blessing.

In the pursuit of God's prosperity in your life, it is imperative that you remember these three points: God is your resource, His abundance is for a purpose larger than yourself, and you must depend on Him as the Blesser rather than seek the blessings—trust Him to supply all you need and beyond, at the perfect time.

Read Psalm 30.

Questions:

David enjoyed great prosperity in the material world. Yet, what was the attitude of David's heart in this Psalm?

✎_____

_____

_____

_____

What can you glean from this Psalm that will enable you to correctly view kingdom prosperity?

✎_____

_____

_____

_____

Record Your Thoughts

How has your view of kingdom prosperity changed as you have studied this session? Write out, in detail, your current view of this topic and how you foresee your future walk in this regard.

✎ _____

_____

_____

_____

Write out a prayer you can pray with confidence, asking God for resources to help you reach where you know He wants you to go in this season of your life.

✎ _____

_____

_____

_____

ADDITIONAL OBSERVATIONS

SESSION ELEVEN

Prayer and Faith

Kingdom Key—*Focus On The Lord*

Isaiah 26:3 You will keep him in perfect peace, whose mind is stayed on You, because he trusts in You.

To those who continually seek the Lord and fervently desire to know His plan and His will, prayer is an effortless and inherent aspect of life. Prayer is heart-to-heart conversation with our Father. Through prayer, we learn of Him; through prayer, we reinforce our realization of His sufficiency and our need; through prayer, we enter into the very presence of our Heavenly Father and find rest for our souls.

It is unity with our Father and His purposes that should be our focus when we come into His presence. However, far too often people pray with other motivations such as physical or financial improvements. It is natural, of course, for us to want to learn "secrets of success." But it may be that our definition of success is contrary to kingdom principles and dynamics. True success in the kingdom is to live our lives in total unity with our Father. (Read John 17:20–26.)

We read in Scripture that we should come "boldly" to our Father (Hebrews 4:16). The term "boldly" gives the connotation of an assertive faith. However, the power of prayer is not found in the assertive faith that seeks to require God to do whatever we may desire; true spiritual power is in the aggressive faith which contends for *the will of God to be done as revealed in the Scriptures.*

In order for this assertive faith to be released in a manner that does not become self-serving, it's crucial we become believers who are fully committed to the agenda of God's Kingdom alone—to His will and His rule. As that commitment becomes true of us, then the promise of Matthew 6:33 becomes truly available to us: "But seek first the kingdom of God and His righteousness, and all these things shall be added to you."

Read Philippians 4:6–7.

Questions:

What kind of thanks does Paul encourage when making prayerful requests?

_____

_____

_____

Does it seem awkward to you to give thanks before you've made a request? Why or why not?

_____

_____

_____

If we are seeking God's will first and foremost, what will characterize our requests?

_____

_____

_____

Word Wealth—*Seek*

Seek, *zeteo* (zee-the'-oh); Strong's #2212: In its good sense, this New Testament word means to seek—as in to worship—after God with all one's heart. In ancient times, when the word was used with a negative connotation, it had the meaning of plotting or scheming. But when the believer seeks after God with the whole heart, strategizing for and welcoming God's Kingdom as an immediate reality, that's when the Lord can "add all these things" which have been desired from the depths of our hearts.

Kingdom Life—*Cast Your Cares*

Peter called for a casting of every care upon the Lord (1 Peter 5:7).The basis for this act of prayer is founded in the knowledge of the Lord's love. That's the starting place—the foundation for praying in faith. Only when we are convinced of the Lord's abiding affection for us—right at the intimate personal dimension of our lives—is it possible for us to come before Him in the simplicity of confident faith.

Jesus knew the difficulty we would experience in seeking to rest in faith, believing that God cares about our needs. The enemy of our prayer life will often suggest that we will not get what we're asking for. You will hear his whisper, "Instead of getting your needs met, something worse will happen—and you deserve it!" But as you allow the truth of God's Word to shape your thinking, you will find yourself receiving Jesus' words; resting while believing that your loving Father will give *only good things* to His children; only blessing, not cursing, to those who pray to Him in faith.

Read Matthew 7:7–11; Luke 11:9–13.

Questions:

Why do you think it often seems difficult to believe we will receive good things?

_____

_____

_____

What things in our lives get in the way of this call to rest in faith?

_____

_____

_____

How will it affect your faith walk to realize that God wants to and will provide us good things? How might living as if this is true change your prayer life?

_____

_____

_____

_____

Word Wealth—*Cares/Casting*

Care, *merimna* (mer'-im-nah); Strong's #3308: This New Testament word means a distraction or worry. This is the word Jesus uses to describe the cares of this life that choke out the seed of God's Word (Matthew 13:22). It is the nagging thought that distracts you from the task at hand. It is the worrying thought that promotes disunity of purpose within, which may be the best definition for worry.

Casting, *epirrhipto* (ep-ir-hrip'-to); Strong's #1977: Actually, this New Testament word has to do with throwing or hurling, a graphic picture of tossing. Casting should not be thought of as laying a care down; it is more like throwing a care away. Perhaps Peter understood how difficult it is to be rid of those cares—those things that divide our minds and hearts. It may take something more than quiet, meditative thought to reach the point of being able to totally cast away your cares!

Kingdom Extra

When Jesus' disciples asked Him to teach them how to pray, Jesus gave them a very simple example. We may be completely confident in using this example as a guide for faith-filled prayer. Let's take a closer look at The Lord's Prayer (Luke 11:2–4 and Matthew 6:9–13)—the guide Jesus gave to lead us to effective, faith-filled prayer.

- **Our Father in heaven, hallowed be Your name.**
  Begin with praise and worship to the Father.

- **Your kingdom come, Your will be done, on earth as it is in heaven.**

  Commit yourself to His kingdom, to His agenda, to His will.

- **Give us day by day our daily bread**

  Trust Him totally for daily provision.

- **Forgive us our sins**

  Confess, and repent of every sin of which you are being convicted.

- **For we also forgive everyone that is indebted to us.**

  Release every grudge; hold no punishing thoughts in your heart. Send away every offense committed against you. Release them from their sin to answer only to God, the righteous Judge.

- **Do not lead us into temptation, but deliver us from the evil one**

  Ask for grace to deal with any weakness of your life that might be prone to surrender to sin, and ask for His delivering power to liberate you from every bondage.

- **For Yours is the kingdom and the power and the glory forever . . .**

  Conclude with praise over everything you have requested. Give Him all the glory.

Keep this pattern in mind as you spend time with the Lord over the next several days. As you do, you will discover your faith rising in a Father God who deserves your worship, whose kingdom commands your commitment, whose will is altogether good and righteous, whose daily provision is promised, whose loving heart doesn't condemn you in your sins, but has made a way for you to deal with those sins—whose love compels you to be as forgiving to others as He has been towards you. You will find faith rising in the One who will never lead you into temptation, but will lead you out of it!

Read Matthew 6:5–8; Matthew 18:19–20; Matthew 26:41; Mark 11:24; Luke 11:5–8; 1 Timothy 2:8.

Questions:

What do you see as the overriding purpose of prayer?

_____

_____

_____

What can you glean from these passages regarding effective prayer?

_____

_____

_____

What most speaks to you in regard to your own prayer life and what steps can you take to improve the quality and effectiveness of your own prayer life?

_____

_____

_____

Word Wealth—*Agree*

Agree, *sumphoneo* (soom-fo-neh'o); Strong's #4856: This New Testament word means to be harmonious, to be in one accord, to stipulate agreement. Our word, "symphony," is derived from this word. *Sumphoneo*—agree—does not imply that the availability of God's *power* is based upon *our* agreement. Rather, when believers are in agreement *about something that is God's will*, this promised power flows directly from the Father.

Kingdom Extra

John chapters 14–16 contain the last words Jesus spoke to His disciples before His ministry on earth was completed—before He returned to His Father and sat at His right side. We can only imagine the urgency and passion in Jesus' voice as He spoke to His disciples (and us) in His last hours with them. Doubtless, the subjects He chose on that fateful night were of primary importance. Powerful messages on prayer and living life in unity with the Father and His will were among the teachings of Jesus on the night he was betrayed.

Read John 14:11–14; John 15:1–7; John 16:2–24. (You may wish to read all three chapters in order to have a fuller understanding of the verses listed here.)

Questions:

Make a list of the subjects about which Jesus taught on this fateful night. Why do you believe He chose these specific subjects?

_____

_____

What do you believe it means to "abide" in Jesus?

_____

_____

What does Jesus mean when He says His Word should abide in you?

_____

_____

How do you believe each of the subjects you listed adds to and perfects a life filled with spiritual authority and fruitfulness in prayer?

_____

_____

What does it mean to pray in the name of Jesus?

_____

_____

Probing the Depths

Today, as in the culture of the biblical languages, "praying in the name of" communicates the concept of representative authority. If someone came in the name of Caesar, it usually meant that they were an appointed envoy of Imperial Rome, with the authority to carry out a specific assignment. This carried much the same dynamics as someone granted the "power of attorney" today—it means that they can execute a matter of business in someone else's name.

To pray in Jesus' name is not to use a mystical term that has magical power in itself. To pray in Jesus' name is not the license to use His authority to accomplish *your* personal objectives. Anyone today using a "power of attorney" in such a self-serving manner may eventually wind up in jail. In ancient Rome, anyone abusing the power of the Imperial court usually wound up dead!

By reason of God's gentle grace, nothing so drastic immediately happens to anyone abusing the power of Jesus' name. We may marvel at the mercy of the Lord in this respect, but let us remember the story in the Book of Acts. Some young men tried to cast out a demon "by Jesus whom Paul preached." The demonized man attacked them and tore their clothes off! Typically, people who attempt to misuse the name discover God's power is available for *God's* will, not *man's.*

Kingdom Life—*Do Not Waver*

In Romans 4:20–21, we read about the strength of Abraham's faith in the face of a seemingly impossible situation. Abraham and Sarah were old, even by today's standards—certainly much too elderly to bear children. However, God had made a promise to Abraham. So Abraham "contrary to hope, in hope believed, so that he became the father of many nations, according to what was spoken" (Romans 4:18). "He did not doubt God's promise, but stood strong in faith. He believed he would receive exactly what God promised. Abraham's faith did not waver."

The word "waver" in Romans 4:20, is translated from the Greek *diakrino* (Strong's #1252; dee-ak-ree'-no) which means: to separate thoroughly, to withdraw from, or to discriminate or hesitate. This is a different word than the word "to judge," but both words contain the Greek word *krino*. On the one hand, we are exhorted to be discerning, while never doubting. We are to investigate a matter thoroughly, but once we have prayerfully committed the matter to God, we are to cease our examination!

Remember this: Once you have decided to pray, it means you have judged *(krino)* the matter to belong to God. To waver *(diakrino)* means that you now wonder if there is something else you are supposed to do, or if this is something God cannot, or will not, do. This is to doubt. It wars against your faith and blocks the release of God's power from answering your prayer. Investigate the matter fully *(anakrino)*; then make a judgment. If you present the matter to God in prayer, leave it there without doubting *(diakrino*—to think it through all over again!).

Read James 1:6; John 20:25–29.

Questions:

Once you've given something to God, do you leave it there? Why or why not?

✎ _____

_____

_____

If you struggle with doubting, what should you do?

✎ _____

_____

What can you learn from Thomas that will serve to increase your ability to walk in faith without *diakrino*?

✎ _____

_____

_____

Kingdom Life—*Pray in Faith*

There are four types of prayers you can pray in faith, even when you are confused or don't understand what God is doing. There is never doubt that these four types of prayers are in line with God's will in our lives. You can always pray these prayers with complete faith that you are in line with the perfect will of God.

1. The Prayer of Surrender

Read: Matthew 26:36–42, Mark 14:32–36, and Luke 22:39–46. Not one of us can understand the agony Jesus was experiencing. Though we struggle against sin, we do not do so from the vantage point of purity as He did. Jesus had never sinned (and never would)—it was not a part of His nature—and so He was in agony as He faced the potential of sin separating Him from the Father, as He was about to take our place in suffering for sin's penalty.

But think of it. Still, He surrendered! In Luke's account, an angel ministered strength to Him (Luke 22:43). Ultimately, He surrendered to the death of the cross. We may conclude that if—as He did—we prayerfully surrender in faith to God's will, we also will be supernaturally strengthened, and ultimately exalted with Christ, as well.

Another great example of the prayer of surrender is found in the words of Mary when, upon hearing Gabriel's declaration, responded, "Let it be to me according to Your word." (Luke 1:38) While the surrender of Jesus was based upon complete knowledge of what was going to happen to Him, Mary had no idea what would become of her commitment. She could not know the pain and sorrow that her future would hold, yet she said, "Let it be to me according to your word."

There are some things you know about your circumstances and some things you know about God's plan for your life. But there are also some future events of which you have no knowledge. With confidence, surrender to Him, to His will, and to His ways. Your decision could possibly carry you through trying times; nonetheless, be like Mary. Reckon God's promise to be true. Know that His power will overshadow you, and that something of His life and power is being born in you—His likeness is being begotten in you increasingly. Knowing these truths, say with confidence, "Let it be to me according to Your Word."

2. The Prayer for Deliverance

As Pat Robertson has said, "It is often important to exercise a key to the miraculous—the spoken word. God has given us authority over disease, demons, sickness, storms, and finances (Matthew 10:1; Luke 10:19). Often, we may keep asking God to act, when, in fact, He calls us to employ His authority by our action with divinely empowered speech. Then we may declare that authority in Jesus' name: we may command needed funds to come to us, command a storm to be stilled, command a demon to come out, command any affliction to leave, command a sickness to depart.

"Jesus said, 'Whoever says to this mountain, "Be removed and be cast into the sea," and does not doubt in his heart, but believes that those things he says will be done, he will have whatever he says' (Mark 11:23). Believe in your heart that it has already happened! With the anointing of faith that God gives you, speak it forth. But remember, miracles come by faith in God's present power, not by a ritual or formula of human works or willpower."

3. The Prayer for Healing

Read James 5:14–15. Just as Exodus 15:26 is called the Old Testament Divine Healing Covenant, James 5:13–18 is viewed as the New Testament Divine Healing Covenant. The inspired apostle affirms that those sick persons whom the elders of the church anoint with oil, and for whom they pray, will be healed.

"The Lord will raise him up" (James 5:15). That's the promise.

4. The Prayer for Revelation

Read Ephesians 1:17. With confidence, you can pray for "revelation." Because this word is being misused in some sections of the church, you may struggle with the idea.

The word 'revelation' is used in two ways in the Bible. It is important to distinguish them, not only to avoid confusion in studying the Word of God, but to assure the avoidance of a destructive detour into humanistic ideas and hopeless error. The Holy Scriptures are called 'the revealed Word of God.' The Bible declares that God's "law" (Deuteronomy 29:29) and the "prophets" (Amos 3:7) are the result of His revealing work, essentially describing the whole of the Old Testament as *"revealed."* In the New Testament this word is used of writings as well (Romans 16:25; Ephesians 3:3; Revelation 1:1)—writings that became part of the closed canon of the Holy Scriptures.

Wisdom and understanding, as well as sound, practical speech, recommend that today's believer both know and clearly express what is meant when he or she speaks of "revelations." The Holy Spirit does indeed give us *revelation,* as this text teaches. But such prophetic insight into the Word should never be considered as equal to the actual giving of the Holy Scriptures. As helpful as insight into God's Word may be, the finality of the *whole* of the revelation of God's Holy Word is the only sure ground for building our lives.

Record Your Thoughts

Faith and prayer are ultimately tools used personally and, most often, privately. It would be of great value in your walk of faith to develop a prayer schedule. Set aside a specific time to pray each day. It won't be long before that scheduled prayer becomes such an integral part of your life, you wouldn't think of missing it.

Write out your prayer schedule for the next month. Taking what you have learned, what adjustments will you make in your prayer style? What corrections will you make to accomplish your goal to pray faithfully and in faith?

SESSION TWELVE

The Father of Faith

 Kingdom Key—*Covenant Partners With God*

Genesis 17:7 . . . I will establish My covenant between Me and you and your descendants after you in their generations, for an everlasting covenant, to be God to you and your descendants after you.

God spoke these words to Abraham. His "descendants . . . in their generations" includes all those who belong to the Lord (Galatians 3:29). We have been "adopted," (Romans 4:4–7) we have been "grafted" (Romans 11:17) into the family tree of Abraham. The Bible calls Abraham the father of those of us who believe (Romans 4:11). He is the one to whom God made the promise, "You will be the father of many nations" (Genesis 17:4), and when Paul writes to the Galatians, he makes the point that *everyone* who believes in Jesus Christ has become an offspring of Abraham (Galatians 3:29). As persons of faith, you and I have become members of the household of Abraham (Romans 4:13), so promises spoken to Abraham's descendants are words that you and I can apply to our own lives of faith (Romans 4:16; Galatians 3:16).

Abraham is a wonderful role model for the life of faith. Abraham was not perfect and certainly made some mistakes, but his faith began the covenant relationship between God and mankind which Jesus has now made available to all of us.

Read 2 Samuel 7:24; Jeremiah 33:24–26; Romans 9:4, 11:2, 29.

Questions:

God has promised to remain in eternal relationship to His people. What words of Jesus mirror this promise? (Matthew 28:20; Hebrews 13:5)

✎ _____

_____

_____

In what ways should this fact impact our faith?

✎ _____

_____

_____

 ## Word Wealth—*Covenant*

Covenant, *berit* (beh-reet′); Strong's #1285: Old Testament word meaning a covenant, compact, pledge, treaty, or agreement. This is one of the most theologically important words in the Bible, appearing more than 250 times in the Old Testament. A *berit* may be made between individuals, between a king and his people, or by God with His people. In the covenant God made with Abraham, God's irrevocable pledge is that He will be God to Abraham and his descendents forever. The greatest provision of the Abrahamic covenant, this is the foundation stone of Israel's eternal relationship to God (2 Samuel 7:24; Jeremiah 33:24–26; Romans 9:4, 11:2, 29). All other Bible promises are based on this one.

Covenant, *diatheke* (dee-ath-ay′-kay); Strong's #1242: Greek word meaning a will, testament, pact, contract—an agreed upon plan to which both parties subscribe. While the word may signify an agreement between two parties, with each accepting mutual obligations, most often it is a declaration of one person's will. In the Bible, God initiated the whole action, set the condition, and defined as a decree a declaration of purposes. In the New Testament, Jesus ratified by His death on the cross a new covenant—"a better covenant" (Hebrews 7:22).

Kingdom Life—*Press On*

In order to prepare for the next few sections of our study, take some time now to read Genesis chapters 12–22. We will take a look at the parallels in Abraham's journey and our own walk of faith.

Genesis 12:1–3: Abram leaves Haran for Canaan because of the Lord's word.

The life of faith involves both our response to a promise, and our leaving of something behind. In Abram's case, he was called to an unidentified land. While he had no idea where his response of faith would finally lead him, it was clear what he was leaving. The journey of faith is often like this. God makes clear only what we are to leave— to discontinue—while the future remains unclear. This doesn't suggest an uncertain future for those who walk by faith, it is merely unclear at times. Certainty is sustained by the Lord's presence and promise, even when we can't see tomorrow.

Abram's obedience in leaving is based on God's clear word of instruction, "Get out of your country, from your family" (Genesis 12:1). Though the Lord only promised to identify the land at some future point, His other promises were quite clear. These same clear promises may be rightly applied in the life of everyone who believes as Abraham did.

You may believe with certainty for the fulfillment of the promises given to Abraham in your own life if you are, with certainty, leaving behind those things which the Lord has clearly addressed. Remember the old saying of the church, "There can be no cleaving (unto the Lord) without leaving (the world)."

Read Philippians 3:12–14; 1 Corinthians 9:24–27.

Questions:

Which things are clear and which remain unclear in your own faith journey?

What do you find it hard to release and leave behind as you continue on your journey of faith?

✎ _____

_____

_____

What does it mean to "press on?"

✎ _____

_____

 ## Kingdom Life—*Overcome the World*

Genesis 12:10 – 13:18: Abram leaves Canaan for Egypt because of a famine.

Even though we believe God and follow His Word and way, we have no guarantee against famines! Our journey of faith—like Abram's—will pass through famines. Such "dry spells" sometimes come in the form of lost jobs, sickness, and/or other modes of suffering. Faith is not a magic power to ward off evil. Faith is the God-given power to process reality. Faith never denies reality but moves through it in confidence toward God's promise of victory. Indeed, 1 John 5:4 specifically announces that faith is the victory that overcomes the world. You win the moment you take a position of faith and decide to put your trust in the Lord—in what He has said in the midst of threatening circumstances.

Some suggest that Abram should not have left the land God had just identified as the land that would be his (Genesis 12:7–9). If this indeed were a failure in Abram's faith—if He failed to trust God in the face of difficult circumstances—it is all the more precious to note how the Lord dealt with his shortcoming. Instead of plaguing Abram for his lack of faith, God plagued the household of Pharaoh. While it does not appear that Abram was in a position to choose to leave Egypt, God intervened in such a way that Abram was provided for and virtually forced to return to the land which would become his.

Rejoice in this. Your journey of faith does not require you to be perfect. A believer is not someone who is faultless. However, a believer is someone who is responsive to God when his faults are discovered. Abram returned to the altar he had made when he first came to the land, and there he called again on the name of the Lord (Genesis 13:3–4).

Here is the lesson: *If you fail to trust God in the face of threatening circumstances, return as quickly as possible to the place where you first called upon Him, and renew your commitment.*

Read Romans 8:35–39; 1 John 5:4–5.

Questions:

When in your own walk of faith have you failed to trust God through trying circumstances?

✎ _____

_____

What was God's response?

✎ _____

_____

How has this impacted your current walk of faith?

✎ _____

_____

 Kingdom Extra

In chapters 13 and 14 of Genesis, we find two lessons to help us on our faith journey:

1. *When the choices of others leave you at a disadvantage, your God has you exactly where He wants you! In the very circumstance that appears to resemble a desert, He will fulfill all the promises He has made.*

   It looked as if Lot's choice of land had garnered him the best, most desirable land. However, Lot's choice left Abram exactly where God wanted him: dependent upon God to fulfill His promises.

It is not uncommon for sincere believers to make the mistake of manipulating their circumstances, of trying to "help" God. Though sincere, these efforts usually "help"—they help bring about the *opposite* results. It's a lesson that every man and woman of faith has to learn.

2. A *person of faith will not permit an association that will tarnish the source of blessing.*

In chapter 14, we read of a rescue, a profound reverence, and a refusal to be partnered with anything or anyone that does not recognize the sovereignty of God. From these accounts, we can learn much about keeping our walk with the Lord pure and undefiled by the world—its values and its ways.

 Kingdom Life—*Believe the Promise Maker*

Genesis 15: Abram's covenant-making sacrifice.

Genesis 15:6 is extraordinary, and became a foundation stone for Paul's teaching on grace and faith in the New Testament.

When Abram complained that he had no heir, God promised He would provide an heir of Abram's seed. God directed Abram to look at the stars and said, "So shall your descendants be." In faith, Abram believed the Lord. Abram's faith made it possible for the Lord to "account" to him righteousness. That means that God, by His grace and choice in love, attributed to Abram's record the full complement of His righteousness and promised justification; just as He will do for us through our Lord, Jesus Christ.

Abram heard the promise and believed in the Lord. As you grow as a person of faith, it will become increasingly important for you to recognize the distinction between believing in *the promise,* and believing in the *One who has made the promise.* For Abram the latter was true. Abram's faith made it possible for the Lord God to account righteousness to him.

Read Jeremiah 23:6; Galatians 3:5–9; Ephesians 2:8; 2 Thessalonians 2:15–17.

Questions:

In what way does God account our belief and faith in Christ as our "righteousness?"

✎ _____

_____

_____

How might one be able to discern the difference in believing the promise rather than believing the One who made the promise?

✎ _____

_____

_____

Have you, in your own walk of faith, made the error of believing the promise rather than the Promise Maker? What has been the result and how can you guard against this in the future?

✎ _____

_____

_____

Probing the Depths

Genesis 16: Abram attempts to fulfill God's promise.

Abram's desire to have a son outweighed his desire to trust God. He attempted to bring about God's promise by his own efforts. Although having a child with his wife's maid was a totally acceptable practice in that ancient time, it was not acceptable for Abram as a man called to faith in God. The result was great anguish for Sarai (Sarah), Hagar, and Abram as God turned His back on the deed borne of unbelief. (God revealed Himself to Hagar as the God who sees all and He committed Himself to care for her and Ishmael, her child.)

Most of us, though people of faith, have given birth to our own "Ishmaels." The name *Ishmael* means "God will hear;" even when we fail in a part of our faith journey, God will still hear! He does not leave us to the results of our fleshly thinking or actions; but he intervenes so the promise He has made can still come to pass in the manner He intends!

 **Kingdom Life—*Wait Upon the Lord***

Genesis 18: Abram becomes Abraham and is promised a son through Sarah.

God changed Abram's name (which means High Father or Patriarch) to Abraham (which means Father of a Multitude). Thus God was arranging that every time Abraham heard his own name, he would be reminded of God's promise. From this, we can glean a kingdom principle: let God's words, which designate His will and promise for your life, become as fixed in your mind and as governing of your speech as Abraham's name change was in shaping his concept of himself. "Faith comes by hearing" (Romans 10:17), so Abraham's faith was strengthened to enable him to continue to believe when God's promise seemed to be endlessly delayed.

Even when it seems God's promises have long been delayed, let His Word so resonate in your heart and mind that your certainty outlives the delay. We see this patient faith clearly in Abraham's journey. We must remember that faith does not operate in an atmosphere of immediacy or convenience. Faith *can* have immediate results; faith *can* even have convenient results. The mistake is to assume the passing of time makes void the promise or that God has decided to permit His promise to be fulfilled through the results of human provision, rather than through His own miraculous power and timing.

Read Isaiah 40:28–31; Psalm 37:3–9; Galatians 5:22–25.

Questions:

What are the promises of Scripture for those who will patiently wait on the timing of God?

✎ _____

_____

_____

In what ways is impatience detrimental to a life of faith?

✎ _____

_____

_____

Describe the person who lives with all the fruit of the spirit in evidence. How do you measure up?

✎ _____

_____

_____

What steps can you take to increase your ability to patiently wait upon the Lord? (Re-read Hebrews 12:2.)

✎ _____

_____

_____

 ## Kingdom Life—*Having Done All, to Stand*

We can be deceived by unbalanced, unbiblical teaching, so our intake of God's Word becomes crucial in cultivating, growing, and evaluating our faith. It is through His Word that faith is made alive (Romans 10:17). And it is with His Word that we fight against the enemy.

Satan seeks to over throw your faith; the focus of his attacks against you will be directed almost exclusively toward your faith—if he can make your faith ineffective, you pose no threat to his evil agenda. We have seen throughout this lesson that faith involves hearing, making choices, repenting, and learning—knowing, choosing, and standing strong in the truth of God. We must be prepared to stand strong in the face of Satan's attacks against our faith.

Read Ephesians 6:10–18; 1 John 5:4; 1 Peter 5:6–10.

Questions:

What are some of the "fiery darts" that Satan uses in your life in his attempt to make your faith ineffective?

_____

_____

_____

_____

In what ways do you see perseverance in your life? Where do you see it lacking? What steps can you take to increase your ability to stand strong in the Lord in the face of trial and difficulty?

_____

_____

_____

_____

In what way do you see this as a critical aspect of living a life of power faith?

_____

_____

_____

_____

Record Your Thoughts

God desires to bring us to the place where we will trust Him on all terms, in every situation, and walk with Him—above and beyond all. This is the overriding truth that all of faith's lessons are intended to engrave upon our souls. Ultimately, when we stand before God, our faith is what will bring Him honor and glory. "That the genuineness of your faith, being much more precious than gold that perishes, though it is tested by fire, may be found to praise, honor, and glory at the revelation of Jesus Christ" (1 Peter 1:7).

Now that you have completed this lesson on power faith, your journey has only begun. Faith is like a muscle that grows and strengthens with use. Toward that end, begin to exercise your faith daily—moment by moment. Keep a notebook handy during prayer times to record your requests of the Lord and the promise on which you stand in that regard. Date your requests and then **wait**. As God answers, record the date you received from His hand. Your faith will grow as you experience the faithfulness of God.

Remember the words of Hebrews 11:6, "without faith *it is* impossible to please *Him*, for he who comes to God must believe that He is, and that He is a rewarder of those who diligently seek Him."

"For I am not ashamed of the gospel of Christ, for it is the power of God to salvation for everyone who believes, for the Jew first and also for the Greek. For in it the righteousness of God is revealed from faith to faith; as it is written, 'The just shall live by faith'" (Romans 1:16–17).

Begin your prayer journal with your thoughts on these last two Scripture portions then continue daily to record your own faith journey into the kingdom expression of Power Faith.

ADDITIONAL OBSERVATIONS